FOU

PATHWAYS

SECOND
EDITION

Listening, Speaking, and Critical Thinking

CYNTHIA FETTIG
KATHY NAJAFI

**NATIONAL
GEOGRAPHIC**
L E A R N I N G

Australia • Brazil • Mexico • Singapore • United Kingdom • United States

NATIONAL GEOGRAPHIC
LEARNING

Pathways Foundations: Listening, Speaking, and Critical Thinking, 2nd Edition

Cynthia Fettig and Kathy Najafi

Publisher: Sherrise Roehr

Executive Editor: Laura Le Dréan

Managing Editor: Jennifer Monaghan

Senior Development Editor: Eve Einselen Yu

Associate Development Editors:
Lisl Bove and Jennifer Williams-Rapa

Director of Global and U.S. Marketing:
Ian Martin

Product Marketing Manager: Tracy Bailie

Media Research: Leila Hishmeh

Senior Director, Production:
Michael Burggren

Manager, Production: Daisy Sosa

Content Project Manager: Mark Rzeszutek

Senior Digital Product Manager: Scott Rule

Manufacturing Planner: Mary Beth
Hennebury

Interior and Cover Design: Brenda
Carmichael

Art Director: Brenda Carmichael

Composition: MPS North America LLC

For product information and technology assistance, contact us at
Cengage Learning Customer & Sales Support, cengage.com/contact

For permission to use material from this text or product,
submit all requests online at **cengage.com/permissions**
Further permissions questions can be emailed to
permissionrequest@cengage.com

Student Edition: 978-1337-40770-0
SE + Online Workbook: 978-1-337-56250-8

National Geographic Learning
20 Channel Center Street
Boston, MA 02210
USA

National Geographic Learning, a Cengage Learning Company, has a mission to bring the world to the classroom and the classroom to life. With our English language programs, students learn about their world by experiencing it. Through our partnerships with National Geographic and TED Talks, students develop the language and skills they need to be successful global citizens and leaders.

Locate your local office at **international.cengage.com/region**

Visit National Geographic Learning online at **NGL.Cengage.com/ELT**
Visit our corporate website at **www.cengage.com**

Printed in China

Print Number: 02   Print Year: 2018

Contents

Scope and Sequence

Speaking & Presentation	Vocabulary	Grammar & Pronunciation	Critical Thinking
• Making Small Talk • Making Eye Contact **Lesson Task** Interviewing a Classmate **Final Task** Giving a Presentation about Yourself	Collocations	• Simple Present and Past of *Be* • Contractions with *Be*	**Focus:** Activating Prior Knowledge Analyzing a Visual, Categorizing, Organizing Ideas, Personalizing, Predicting, Previewing, Reflecting
• Using Listing Words • Closing a Presentation **Lesson Task** Discussing Different Types of Jobs **Final Task** Presenting your Dream Job	Antonyms	• Simple Present • Simple Present *-s* Form of the Verb	**Focus:** Categorizing Information Analyzing, Interpreting, Organizing Ideas, Personalizing, Predicting, Previewing, Prior Knowledge, Reflecting, Synthesizing
• Agreeing and Disagreeing • Presenting with Graphics **Lesson Task** Planning a Vacation for your Teacher **Final Task** Presenting Class Survey Results	Synonyms	• Present Continuous • Syllables and Stress	**Focus:** Thinking about Pros and Cons Analyzing, Categorizing, Interpreting, Making Inferences, Personalizing, Predicting, Prior Knowledge, Synthesizing
• Giving Reasons • Getting People's Attention **Lesson Task** Presenting a New Tech Device **Final Task** Presenting a New App	Adjective Order	• *Can* and *Can't* • *Can* and *Can't*	**Focus:** Interpreting a Bar Graph Analyzing, Applying, Brainstorming, Evaluating, Interpreting, Judging, Personalizing, Synthesizing

Scope and Sequence

Speaking & Presentation	Vocabulary	Grammar & Pronunciation	Critical Thinking
• Giving Examples • Asking for Questions **Lesson Task** Presenting a Personal Plan **Final Task** Telling a Story	Noun Suffixes -er and -ing	• Simple Past • Simple Past -ed Endings	**Focus:** Paraphrasing Brainstorming, Evaluating, Interpreting a Chart, Organizing Ideas, Personalizing, Previewing, Ranking, Reflecting
• Giving Sources of Information • Using Photos for Emphasis and Effect **Lesson Task** Presenting a Project Plan **Final Task** Presenting a Project Using Images	Prefixes: re- and un-	• Future with *Be Going To* • Future with *Will* • *Be Going To (Gonna)*	**Focus:** Understanding Bias Analyzing Results, Brainstorming, Categorizing, Evaluating, Organizing Ideas, Personalizing, Predicting, Previewing, Prior Knowledge, Synthesizing
• Saying Years Correctly • Body Language **Lesson Task** Talking about Your Life **Final Task** Presenting a Personal History	Using a Dictionary to Find a Word Form	• *Wh-* Questions in the Simple Past • *Wh-* Question Intonation	**Focus:** Recalling Information Brainstorming, Organizing Ideas, Personalizing, Predicting, Previewing, Reflecting, Synthesizing
• Expressing Opinions • Using Questions **Lesson Task** Group Debates on Cloning **Final Task** Group Presentation: DNA in the Real World	Two-Part Verbs	• Modals of Possibility: *Could, May, Might,* and *Will* • Schwa /ə/ in Unstressed Syllables	**Focus:** Considering Other Opinions Analyzing Visuals, Brainstorming, Evaluating, Organizing Ideas, Personalizing, Predicting, Prior Knowledge, Reflecting

Introduction to *Pathways*

Pathways Listening, Speaking, and Critical Thinking, Second Edition

uses compelling National Geographic stories, photos, video, and infographics to bring the world to the classroom. Authentic, relevant content and carefully sequenced lessons engage learners while equipping them with the skills needed for academic success.

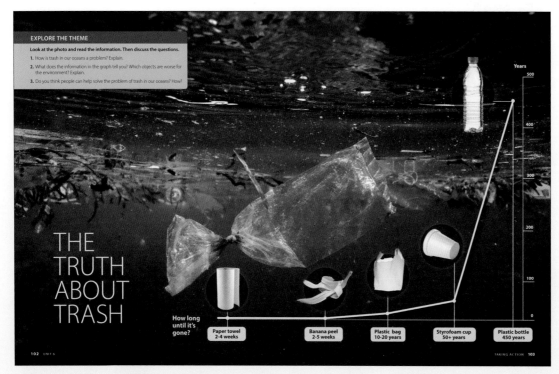

Explore the Theme provides a visual introduction to the unit, engaging learners academically and encouraging them to share ideas about the unit theme.

NEW Integrated listening and speaking activities help **prepare students for standardized tests** such as IELTS and TOEFL.

UPDATED *Video* sections use relevant National Geographic **video clips** to give learners another perspective on the unit theme and further practice of listening and critical thinking skills.

Listening Skills

B Listening A Conversation about a Vacation

BEFORE LISTENING

PREDICTING **A** Look at the photo and read the caption. What do you think you will hear about this place? Discuss your prediction with a partner.

WHILE LISTENING

LISTENING FOR MAIN IDEAS **B** 1.33 Read the question and answer choices. Then listen to the conversation and choose the correct answer.

What did Maria think about her trip to the ICEHOTEL?
a. It was an amazing manmade place, but she didn't like the cold.
b. It was a place with a good mix of natural and manmade.
c. It was crowded with too many tourists.

Visitors in front of the Jukkasjärvi ICEHOTEL in northern Sweden

56 UNIT 3 LESSON B

NOTE-TAKING SKILL Using a ...

One way to listen and take notes is to listen for the answers to questions. This will help you understand the main ideas. When you listen to a story or a conversation, use a wh-question chart. Note the answers to questions like the ones in this chart.

Who?	Who are the important people?
Whaт?	What happens?
Where?	Where does it happen?
When?	When does it happen?
Why?	Why does something happen?
How?	How does something happen?

C 1.38 Listen to the conversation again and take notes in the chart. Compare your charts in a small group and add information to your chart. NOTE TAKING

Who?	Maria is talking to Juan about her vacation.
What?	
Where?	
When?	
Why?	
How?	

AFTER LISTENING

D Read the statements. Check (✓) the statements that you think are true. Then compare your answers with a partner. Explain your reasons for your answers. CRITICAL THINKING: MAKING INFERENCES

1. _____ Maria goes to the ICEHOTEL every year.
2. _____ Maria likes to go to unknown places.
3. _____ The ICEHOTEL is open all year.
4. _____ You need warm clothes inside the ICEHOTEL.
5. _____ Maria's friends prefer normal vacations.

UNUSUAL DESTINATIONS 57

NEW *Vocabulary Skills* help students develop essential word building tools such as understanding collocations, word forms, and connotation.

Listening passages incorporate a variety of listening types such as podcasts, lectures, interviews, and conversations.

B Listening A Lecture on Ending Blindness

BEFORE LISTENING

PREDICTING **A** Read the questions and choose your predictions.

1. About how many blind people are there in the world?
   a. 1 out of 20   b. 1 out of 200   c. 1 out of 2,000
2. Which countries have more blindness?
   a. low income   b. high income
3. Is all blindness easy to fix now?
   a. yes   b. no

WHILE LISTENING

LISTENING FOR MAIN IDEAS **B** 2.38 ▶ 1.15 Listen to the first part of the lecture. Choose the correct answers.

NEW *Slide shows* for selected listening passages integrate text and visuals to give learners a more authentic listening experience.

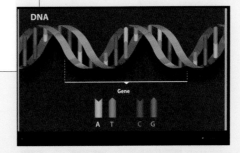

DNA

Gene

A T   C G

UPDATED Explicit listening skill instruction and practice prepares students to listen and take notes in academic settings.

NOTE-TAKING SKILL Using a Timeline

In lesson A, you used a timeline to help you present information. Timelines are also a good way to organize your notes as you listen. You can write dates and important information on the timeline to organize the events in history or in a story.

D 2.29 Listen again and complete the timeline with the important dates and information from the museum tour.

century
or year _____

event

LISTENING SKILL Listening for Signposts

When speakers list something, they usually use signpost words. These words and phrases tell the listener there will be a new idea. Some specific signpost words and phrases to listen for are:
First… Second… Third…
One reason… Another point…
Also…
The last thing…

D 1.19 Listen for the signposts in the excerpt from the lecture. Notice the information after each signpost. Complete it with the words you hear.

1. One thing that many people look for: a job that _____.
2. Another thing people want from a job is to _____.
3. Also, people want their boss to _____.
4. Finally, people want to have _____.

ix

Speaking and Presentation Skills

Speaking lessons guide learners from controlled practice to a final speaking task while reinforcing speaking skills, grammar for speaking, and key pronunciation points.

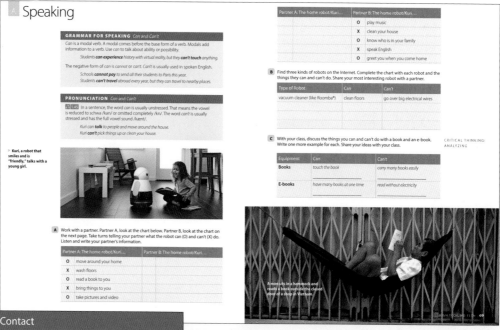

A Speaking

GRAMMAR FOR SPEAKING *Can and Can't*

Can is a modal verb. A modal comes before the base form of a verb. Modals add information to a verb. Use *can* to talk about ability or possibility.

*Students **can experience** history with virtual reality, but they **can't touch** anything.*

The negative form of *can* is *cannot* or *can't*. *Can't* is usually used in spoken English.

*Schools **cannot pay** to send all their students to Paris this year.*
*Students **can't travel** abroad every year, but they can travel to nearby places.*

PRONUNCIATION *Can and Can't*

1.45 In a sentence, the word *can* is usually unstressed. That means the vowel is reduced to schwa /kən/ or omitted completely /kn/. The word *can't* is usually stressed and has the full vowel sound /kænt/.

*Kuri can **talk** to people and move around the house.*
*Kuri **can't** pick things up or clean your house.*

> Kuri, a robot that smiles and is "friendly," talks with a young girl.

A Work with a partner. Partner A, look at the chart below. Partner B, look at the chart on the next page. Take turns telling your partner what the robot can (O) and can't (X) do. Listen and write your partner's information.

Partner A: The home robot/Kuri...	
O	move around your home
X	wash floors
O	read a book to you
X	bring things to you
O	take pictures and video

Partner A: The home robot/Kuri...		Partner B: The home robot/Kuri...	
		O	play music
		X	clean your house
		O	know who is in your family
		X	speak English
		O	greet you when you come home

B Find three kinds of robots on the Internet. Complete the chart with each robot and the things they can and can't do. Share your most interesting robot with a partner.

Type of Robot	Can	Can't
vacuum cleaner (like Roomba®)	clean floors	go over big electrical wires

C With your class, discuss the things you can and can't do with a book and an e-book. Write one more example for each. Share your ideas with your class.

CRITICAL THINKING: ANALYZING

Equipment	Can	Can't
Books	touch the book	carry many books easily
E-books	have many books at one time	read without electricity

A man sits in a hammock and reads a book outside the closed door of a shop in Vietnam.

HIGH-TECH, NO TECH 69

PRESENTATION SKILL Making Eye Contact

Looking at your audience is very important. Making eye contact shows that you are interested in them. They will listen more closely. Follow these tips:

- Look at the audience's faces (the tops of the heads may be easier at first).
- Look around the audience (not at just one person or one side of the room).

Presentation skills such as starting strong, using specific details, making eye contact, pausing, and summarizing, help learners develop confidence and fluency in communicating ideas.

A **Final Task** allows learners to consolidate their understanding of content, language, and skills as they collaborate on an academic presentation.

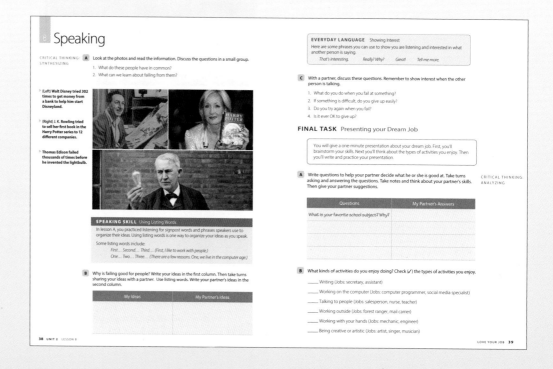

B Speaking

CRITICAL THINKING: SYNTHESIZING

A Look at the photos and read the information. Discuss the questions in a small group.

1. What do these people have in common?
2. What can we learn about failing from them?

> (Left) Walt Disney tried 302 times to get money from a bank to help him start Disneyland.

> (Right) J. K. Rowling tried to sell her first book in the Harry Potter series to 12 different companies.

> Thomas Edison failed thousands of times before he invented the lightbulb.

SPEAKING SKILL Using Listing Words

In lesson A, you practiced listening for signpost words and phrases speakers use to organize their ideas. Using listing words is one way to organize your ideas as you speak.

Some listing words include:

First... Second... Third... (First, I like to work with people.)
One... Two... Three... (There are a few reasons. One, we live in the computer age.)

B Why is failing good for people? Write your ideas in the first column. Then take turns sharing your ideas with a partner. Use listing words. Write your partner's ideas in the second column.

My Ideas	My Partner's Ideas

EVERYDAY LANGUAGE Showing Interest

Here are some phrases you can use to show you are listening and interested in what another person is saying.

That's interesting.   Really? Why?   Great!   Tell me more.

C With a partner, discuss these questions. Remember to show interest when the other person is talking.

1. What do you do when you fail at something?
2. If something is difficult, do you give up easily?
3. Do you try again when you fail?
4. Is it ever OK to give up?

FINAL TASK Presenting your Dream Job

You will give a one-minute presentation about your dream job. First, you'll brainstorm your skills. Next you'll think about the types of activities you enjoy. Then you'll write and practice your presentation.

A Write questions to help your partner decide what he or she is good at. Take turns asking and answering the questions. Take notes and think about your partner's skills. Then give your partner suggestions.

CRITICAL THINKING: ANALYZING

Questions	My Partner's Answers
What is your favorite school subject? Why?	

B What kinds of activities do you enjoy doing? Check (✓) the types of activities you enjoy.

_____ Writing (Jobs: secretary, assistant)
_____ Working on the computer (Jobs: computer programmer, social media specialist)
_____ Talking to people (Jobs: salesperson, nurse, teacher)
_____ Working outside (Jobs: forest ranger, mail carrier)
_____ Working with your hands (Jobs: mechanic, engineer)
_____ Being creative or artistic (Jobs: artist, singer, musician)

SAME AND DIFFERENT 1

These 20-year-old women are at a Coming-of-Age ceremony in Tokyo, Japan.

ACADEMIC SKILLS

LISTENING	Listening for Main Ideas
	Using a Venn Diagram
SPEAKING	Making Small Talk
	Contractions with *Be*
CRITICAL THINKING	Activating Prior Knowledge

THINK AND DISCUSS

1 When you "come of age", you are not a child anymore. In Japan, this happens at age 20. What is the age in your country?

2 Look at the women in the photo. What about them is the same? What is different?

3 Is there a special ceremony for coming-of-age in your country? Is it the same or different from your classmates?

Look at the photos and information. Then discuss the questions.

1. Name the sports on the page. Which sport do people love most around the world? Is this the same or different in your country?

2. How are these sports the same? How are they different?

3. What sports do you like to play? What sports do your classmates like to do or play? What are reasons for the differences?

DO WE LOVE THE SAME SPORTS?

A girl plays soccer at a school in Al Seeb, Oman.

SOCCER
Number of fans:
4 billion

CRICKET
Number of fans:
2.5 billion

A man plays basketball on the beach in the Philippines.

A Cook Islander swings at a ball in a game of cricket in the Cook Islands, New Zealand.

BASKETBALL
Number of fans:
2.2 billion

A Vocabulary

A 🎧 **1.2** Listen and check (✓) the words you already know. Then discuss their meaning with a partner. Check the dictionary for any words you are not sure about.

☐ favorite *(adj)*   ☐ hobby *(n)*   ☐ music *(n)*   ☐ shy *(adj)*

☐ friendly *(adj)*   ☐ kind *(n)*   ☐ science *(n)*   ☐ vacation *(n)*

MEANING FROM CONTEXT

B 🎧 **1.3** Complete Abdul's and Claudia's introduction with the words in exercise A. Then listen and check your answers.

Hi, I am Abdul. I'm from Saudi Arabia. I speak Arabic. I also speak English. I like all sports. My _____ sport is soccer.
       1
I like to listen to rock _____
                 2
and jazz. My favorite school subject is
_____. I am very _____. I
   3   4
like to laugh and have fun.

Hi, I am Claudia, and I'm from Brazil. I speak Portuguese and English. In my country, volleyball is popular. I play volleyball on my school team. My favorite _____ of
                       5
music is pop. My _____ is reading.
              6
I read two books each week! I am
_____ and like to spend time alone. I
   7
love to go to the beach on _____.
                       8

C Write the correct word from exercise A next to its definition.

1. _____ days or weeks away from home, to relax or travel

2. _____ the study of natural things

3. _____ sounds put together (e.g., jazz, classical, pop)

4. _____ one of many different (e.g., soccer is one of many sports)

5. _____ helpful, nice, easy to talk to

6. _____ most liked; more liked than others

7. _____ not liking to talk to people; often quiet

8. _____ an activity such as reading or painting that someone does for fun

D Complete the chart by finding examples of each category in exercise B. Then add other words you know. Compare your chart with a partner.

Country	Language	Sport	Hobby	Music
Saudi Arabia		soccer		

VOCABULARY SKILL Collocations

A collocation is two or more words that often go together. They sound natural together. Certain nouns go with certain verbs. You *speak* a language; you do not *say* a language. You *give* a presentation; you do not *say* a presentation. When you learn a new noun, notice the verb that goes with it and write it in a vocabulary notebook.

Common Verb + Noun Collocations

listen to… *music, the radio, a podcast*

do… *judo, yoga, karate, housework, homework*

play… *a sport, soccer, volleyball, tennis, basketball, cricket, video games, music*

go… *swimming, hiking, running, shopping*

watch… *TV, videos, movies, a game*

E Work with a partner. Read the conversations and choose the correct words. Then practice the conversations.

A: Hi! What do you do in your free time?

B: I (1) (do / play) soccer and (2) (listen to / hear) music. How about you?

A: I (3) (watch / see) TV and (4) (do / go) shopping.

A: What other languages do you (5) (say / speak)?

B: I speak English and Arabic.

A: Do you (6) (go / play) a sport?

B: Yes. I (7) (play / do) karate. How about you?

A: I don't like sports, but I like to (8) (ride / go) bicycles and (9) (do / go) hiking.

F With your partner, practice the conversations in exercise E but use your own personal information.

A Listening A Lecture on Twins

BEFORE LISTENING

PREVIEWING   **A** Look at the photo. These men are identical twins. How are they the same? How are they different? Tell your class.

CRITICAL THINKING   Activating Prior Knowledge

Often you already know information about a topic. Before a class or any discussion, think about the topic. Ask yourself: *What do I already know?* This will help you prepare and be ready for the class or discussion. You will be able to share your ideas more easily.

PRIOR KNOWLEDGE   **B** What do you already know about twins? Discuss the questions with a partner.

1. How are identical twins the same? How are they different?
2. How are identical twins different from fraternal twins?

WHILE LISTENING

LISTENING FOR MAIN IDEAS   **C** 🎧 1.4 ▶ 1.1 Listen to the lecture. Then look at your answers from exercise B. Tell your partner any new information you learned.

LISTENING FOR DETAILS   **D** 🎧 1.5 Listen to the excerpt from the lecture. The professor discusses the "Jim twins." Check (✓) the three facts the professor mentions.

1. _____ The two boys lived with different families.

2. _____ They are both five feet tall.

3. _____ Their wives were named Linda and Betty.

4. _____ They were both firefighters.

5. _____ They both like sports.

6. _____ They both had cats named Toy.

7. _____ They both named a son James.

8. _____ They are both 39 years old now.

One way to organize your notes when you compare two things is to make a Venn diagram. A Venn diagram shows you the things that are the same and the things that are different. Write the things that are the same in the middle area of the two circles. Write the things that are different in the outside areas. Look at the example Venn diagram of the "Jim Twins."

Jim Springer   **Both**   **Jim Lewis**

Springer   Jim   Lewis

E 🎧 1.6 Listen to the excerpt and take notes in the Venn diagram. Write at least two more things that are different and two more things that are the same about the Jim twins. Then compare your diagram with a partner. Add to your notes.

NOTE TAKING

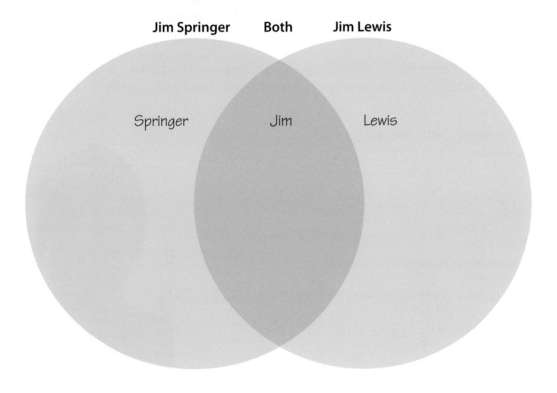

Jim Springer   **Both**   **Jim Lewis**

Springer   Jim   Lewis

AFTER LISTENING

F Discuss the questions with a small group.

CRITICAL THINKING: REFLECTING

1. What surprised you about the Jim twins? Name two things. Explain.

2. How is life difficult (or easy) for twins? Think about school, hobbies, family, friends, and so on.

A Speaking

GRAMMAR FOR SPEAKING Simple Present and Past of *Be*

Be is the most common verb in English and has many forms. Contractions are common when speaking.

Simple Present	Contractions	
Subject + **be (not)**	Affirmative	Negative
I **am (not)** from Saudi Arabia. He/She/It **is (not)** friendly. You/We/They **are (not)** Japanese.	**I'm** She**'s** We**'re**	**I'm not** She**'s not**/She **isn't** We**'re not**/We **aren't**
Simple Past	Contractions	
I/He/She/It **was (not)** in the room. You/We/They **were (not)** cold.	He **wasn't** You **weren't**	

A 🎧 1.7 Complete the information. Use the simple present or simple past of *be*. Write contractions when you hear them. Then listen and check your answers.

MEET CHRIS BASHINELLI

There _____are_____ many National Geographic
                    1

Explorers. This _____is_____ Chris Bashinelli. His
                      2

nickname _____is_____ "Bash." He _____was_____
            3   4

born in New York. His parents _____are were_____ his
                                       5

heroes. They taught him to travel and learn about

the world.

In the past, Chris _____was_____ an actor, but he
                        6

_____isn't_____ (not) an actor now. It was fun, but it _____wasn't_____ (not) the job
        7   8

for him. He wanted to travel and see the world, so he went to Tanzania. Many people

in Tanzania _____are_____ very poor, but they _____aren't_____ (not) unhappy.
                  9   10

Chris learned that you don't need to have a lot of money to have a good life.

The trip changed his life. Now he _____is_____ a storyteller. He has a show on
                                          11

TV (National Geographic Channel). Chris's show is *Bridge the Gap*. It _____is_____
                                                                              12

on TV in over 100 countries around the world!

B Look at the examples of Chris Bashinelli's life in the past and now. Then complete your own chart. Tell the class how you are different now.

PERSONALIZING

Chris Bashinelli's Past	Now
He was born in New York.	He is a world traveler.
He was an actor.	He is a storyteller.

My Past	Now

C 🎧 1.8 Listen and complete the conversation with the form of *be* you hear. Write contractions when you hear them.

A: Hi, I ___am___(1) Muhammad. This ___is___(2) my friend Samir. What ___is___(3) your name?

B: My name ___is___(4) Miguel. ___Are___(5) you two from here?

C: No. We ___are not___(6) Americans. We ___are___(7) from the United Arab Emirates. Where ___are___(8) you from?

B: I ___am___(9) from California. ___Are___(10) you guys students?

A: We ___were___(11) students last year, but now we ___are___(12) teachers. ___Are___(13) you a student?

B: No. I ___was___(14) a student many years ago, but now I ___am___(15) a teacher, too.

C: Well, it ___was___(16) nice to meet you, Miguel.

D Work in a group of three. Check your answers to exercise C. Then take turns practicing the conversation. Use your personal information in the conversation.

A: *Hi, I'm Boris. This is my friend Daria. What's your name?*
B: *My name is Maria. ...*

Small talk is a good way to start talking to someone. Some common topics for small talk are the weather, jobs, hobbies, and sports. Here are some questions you can use to begin small talk.

Job: *What do you do? / Are you a student?*

Hobby: *What do you do in your free time? / Do you have any hobbies?*

Sports: *Do you play any sports?*

Weather: *How do you like this weather? / Can you believe this weather?*

To get the other person to answer the question after you answer it, say *How about you?*

E 🎧 1.9 Complete the conversations with questions from the box. Then listen and check your answers.

Can you believe this weather?	What are your hobbies?	Where are you from?
Do you play any sports?	What do you do?	How about you?

Conversation 1: In class

A: I am from China. _Where are you from?_
                                      1

B: I'm from Australia. _What do you do?_
                                       2

A: I'm a student. _How about you?_
                                3

B: I'm a writer.

A: It's nice to meet you.

B: Nice to meet you, too.

Conversation 2: In an elevator

A: _Can you believe this weather?_ It's so cold.
                              4

B: Tell me about it! Yesterday was so nice!

Conversation 3: At a party

A: Hi. I'm Yoko. And you're Nadia, right?

B: Yes.

A: _Do you play any sports?_
                          5

B: Yes. I play tennis, and I also do judo.

A: That's great. I don't play sports, but I have a lot of hobbies.

B: _What are your hobbies?_
                        6

A: I read books and play chess.

F Practice the conversations from exercise E with a partner. Then switch roles and practice them again.

LESSON TASK Interviewing a Classmate

A Complete the survey with your own answers. Then find a new partner and ask the questions. Write your partner's answers in the chart.

	You	Your Partner
1. How old are you?		
2. Where are you from?		
3. What do you do?		
4. What are your hobbies?		
5. Do you play any sports?		
6. What music do you listen to?		
7. What movies do you watch?		

B How are you and your partner the same? How are you different? Complete the Venn diagram with things that are same and different about you and your partner.

ORGANIZING IDEAS

You _Adriana_   Both   Partner _Mauro_

You:
Calm
taciturn or
reticent
long hair
short
brown eyes
clumsy

Both:
Married
like beach
dogs
sail
swim
paddle
cooking
Watch
Sports

Partner:
Kinetic/hyperactive.
talkative
little bald
tall
green eyes.
graceful

Similarities

C Work with another pair. Use your Venn diagram from exercise B. One partner tells about the things that are the same, and the other partner tells about things that are different.

PRESENTING

> *We have a lot of things in common. We like to play sports. We listen to the same kind of music. We are shy. We have two brothers.*

> *We have some differences, too. She likes to play golf, but I play tennis. Her favorite food is pizza. My favorite food is sushi. Her hobby is reading books. I like to go hiking.*

Video

Coming of Age

A Fulani boy on a journey to become a man

BEFORE VIEWING

A Match each word with its definition.

1. _____ become an adult   a. *(n)* a long trip
2. _____ journey   b. *(v)* be afraid
3. _____ take care of   c. *(v)* have parties, ceremonies, and other festivities
4. _____ worry   d. *(v)* grow from young to older
5. _____ celebrate   e. *(v)* give love and food; protect

PRIOR KNOWLEDGE   **B** What do different cultures do when children "come of age"? Check (✓) the ways you know about.

_____ have a party or dance

_____ receive a gift, such as jewelry

_____ do something painful or dangerous

_____ vote or drive a car

_____ go to a ceremony; wear special clothes

_____ other _____

C Work with a partner. Share your answers to exercise B.

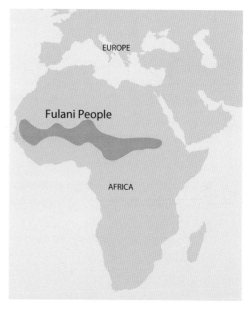

EUROPE

Fulani People

AFRICA

D In the video, you will learn about a Fulani boy from Africa named Yoro. Look at the photo and read the caption. What do you think Fulani boys need to do before they become adults? Discuss your prediction with your partner.

PREDICTING

WHILE VIEWING

E ▶ 1.2 Watch the video. Was your prediction in exercise D correct? Tell your class.

UNDERSTANDING MAIN IDEAS

F ▶ 1.2 Read the statements. Then watch the video again and mark each statement **T** for *True* or **F** for *False*.

UNDERSTANDING DETAILS

1. Yoro walked for only three months.   **T**   **F**

2. The boys take the journey to find water for their cows.   **T**   **F**

3. Girls take the journey also.   **T**   **F**

4. The boys don't have much food and usually only drink milk.   **T**   **F**

5. If the cows look good, then Yoro will be a man.   **T**   **F**

AFTER VIEWING

G Compare your life with Yoro's life. How are you the same and how are you different?

ORGANIZING IDEAS

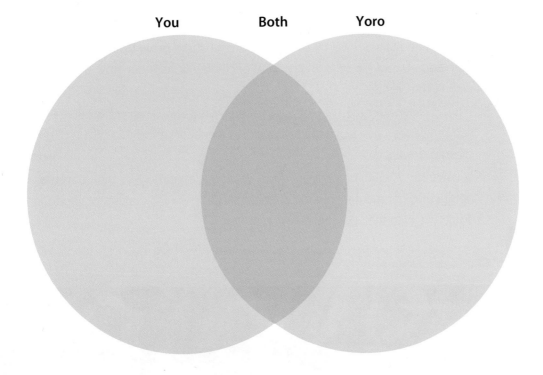

You   Both   Yoro

H Work with a partner. Discuss the questions.

PERSONALIZING

1. How does your country or family celebrate coming of age? How is the celebration different for boys and for girls?

2. What did you do when you became an adult? Or what will you do when you become an adult?

B Vocabulary

A 🎧 1.10 Listen and check (✓) the words you already know.

☐ adult *(n)*   ☐ grow up *(v)*   ☐ teenager *(n)*   ☐ the world *(n)*
☐ change *(v)*   ☐ parents *(n)*   ☐ typical *(adj)*   ☐ years old *(adj)*

MEANING FROM
CONTEXT

B 🎧 1.11 Guess the correct answers to the quiz. Notice each word or phrase in **blue** and think about its meaning. Then listen and check your answers.

QUIZ: HOW TYPICAL ARE YOU?

The world now has seven billion people. What is a **typical** person? Are you typical? Or are you different? *Typical* means different things in every country. Take the quiz. Your opinion of what *typical* means may **change**.

1. A typical size man in Holland is (5'5" / 5'7" / 5'11") tall*, but a typical size man in Peru is (5'3" / 5'4" / 5' 6").

2. A typical Japanese woman lives to be (75 / 81 / 86) **years old**, but a typical woman from Afghanistan lives to be (45 / 52 / 60) years old.

3. A child becomes an **adult** in Saudi Arabia and Indonesia at (15 / 18 / 20) years old, but in the United Arab Emirates and Singapore, the age is (18 / 20 / 21).

4. In the United States, (56 / 69 / 75) percent of children **grow up** in families with both parents, but (78 / 81 / 87) percent of children from India grow up in families with both parents.

5. A typical **teenager** (13–19 years old) in the United States sends (23 / 30 / 41) text messages a day, but a typical Japanese teenager sends (92 / 95 / 100) text messages every day.

6. In Italy, (60 / 70 / 80) percent of young adults live at home with their **parents** before they get married, but in Canada, only (30 / 40 / 50) percent of young adults live with their parents before marriage.

*Note: The United States uses feet (') and inches (") to measure height. To calculate: 1 foot = 12 inches = 30.48 cm. A 5' person is 1.52 meters.

C Write each word or phrase from exercise A next to its definition.

1. _____ a fully-grown person
2. _____ to become different
3. _____ a person between 13 and 19 years old
4. _____ to become an adult, or get older
5. _____ like others; usual
6. _____ a mother and father; people who take care of you
7. _____ the Earth
8. _____ age

D How are you the same as, and how are you different from, the typical people described in exercise B? First complete the chart. Then share it with a partner.

PERSONALIZING

Quiz: Are you typical?	Your Answers
1. How tall are you?	
2. How old is your oldest family member?	
3. At what age do you become an adult in your country?	
4. Did you grow up with both parents?	
5. How many text messages do you send a day?	
6. Are you still living with your parents?	

E Discuss the questions with your partner.

CRITICAL THINKING: REFLECTING

1. The quiz states: "Your opinion of what *typical* means may change." Did your opinion change? If so, how did it change? What does *typical* really mean?

2. Which quiz answers surprised you? Explain.

3. Is it normal for young adults in your country to live at home with their parents? What is good about this? What is difficult about this?

▼ **Crowds of people walk across a street in Osaka, Japan.**

Listening A Conversation about the Teenage Brain

BEFORE LISTENING

PRIOR KNOWLEDGE

A How are teenagers different from adults? Make a list for each. Share your answers with your class.

Teenagers	Adults
no stress about money more emotional	stress about money more responsibility

CRITICAL THINKING: ANALYZING A VISUAL

B Look at the illustration of the teenage brain. Mark each statement T for *True* or F for *False*.

1. A teenager's brain is the same as an adult's brain.　　　　T　　(F)

2. Teenagers have many feelings and emotions because they use the amygdala part of the brain more than adults.　(T)　　F

3. Adults are better at planning because they use the frontal cortex more than teenagers.　(T)　　F

INSIDE A TEEN BRAIN

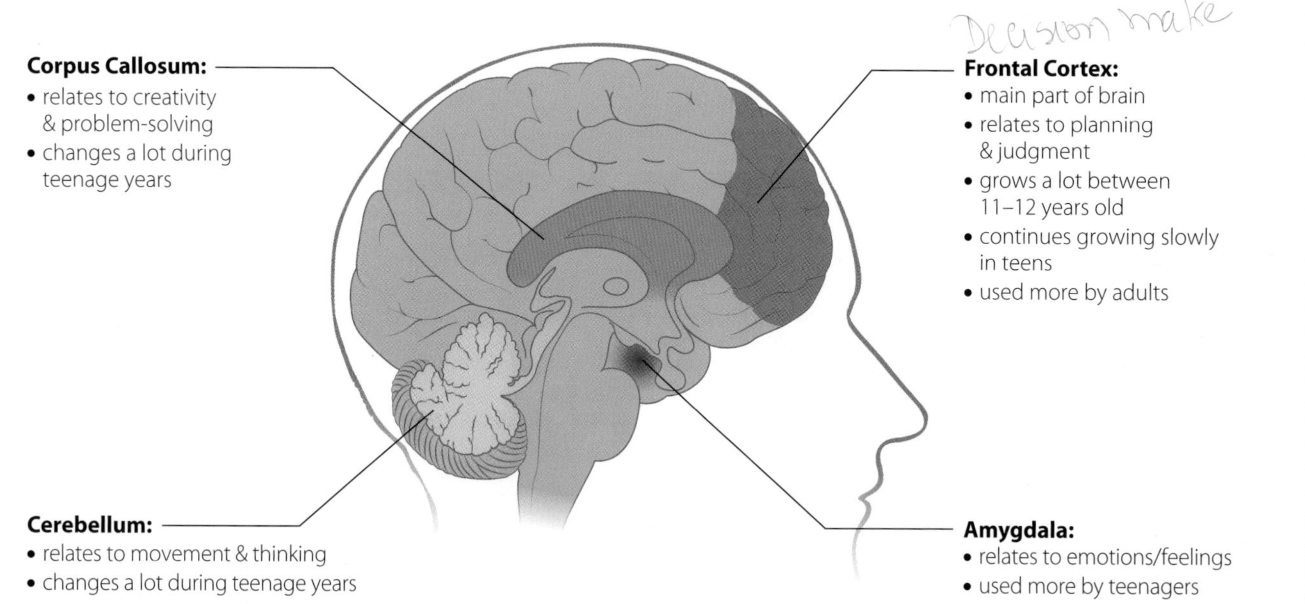

Corpus Callosum:
- relates to creativity & problem-solving
- changes a lot during teenage years

Cerebellum:
- relates to movement & thinking
- changes a lot during teenage years

Decision make

Frontal Cortex:
- main part of brain
- relates to planning & judgment
- grows a lot between 11–12 years old
- continues growing slowly in teens
- used more by adults

Amygdala:
- relates to emotions/feelings
- used more by teenagers

WHILE LISTENING

> **LISTENING SKILL** Listening for Main Ideas
>
> *Main ideas* are a speaker's most important thoughts or ideas. Often a speaker will repeat important words several times. These key words give information about the main idea.
>
> Listen for key words to better understand the main ideas.

Handwritten annotations in top and right margins:

"The grass is always greener on the other side"

You have good taste in clothes (style, your preference).

or

You have bad taste in clothes (style, your prefe.)

C 🎧 1.12 Listen to the conversation. Choose the correct answers.

LISTENING FOR
MAIN IDEAS

1. Pedro is writing a paper about
   a. the teenage body
   b. teenagers
   c. the front part of the brain

2. Which two main ideas does the professor talk about? Choose two answers.
   a. the teenage brain is not fully grown yet
   b. teenagers are difficult people
   c. teenagers cry a lot
   d. writing in a journal helps teenagers
   e. things that impact or change a teenager and how to help

D 🎧 1.12 Listen again. Write three key words.

LISTENING FOR
MAIN IDEAS

_____

_____

_____

E 🎧 1.13 Listen to part of the conversation again. Check the four main things that impact a teenager, according to the professor.

LISTENING FOR
DETAILS

☐ teachers   ☐ experiences   ☐ family   ☐ school
☐ science   ☐ friends   ☐ pets   ☐ media

AFTER LISTENING

F Read and think about the questions. Then work in a group of three or four. Discuss the questions with your group.

CRITICAL THINKING:
REFLECTING

1. What do you think impacts a teenager the most? Explain your answer.

2. How do you think teenagers today are different from teenagers in the past?

3. In the conversation, the professor says, "Tell them that their feelings are typical for a teenager. It is how we grow up. Tell them to write their feelings in a diary or a journal. This may help them understand their feelings more. Also, tell them to talk with their parents and their family, the people who love them." Do you agree with these ideas? Do you have another idea?

B Speaking

PRONUNCIATION Contractions with *Be*

🎧 1.14 Contractions of *be* are common. Listen and say the sentences aloud.

I**'m** a teenager.	I**'m** not an adult.
You**'re** 16 years old?	You **aren't** 15?/You**'re not** 15?
It**'s** typical K-pop music.	It **isn't** the kind of music I like.
She **wasn't** a typical teenager.	They **weren't** typical teenagers.

A 🎧 1.15 Listen and choose the sentence your hear. Then practice saying both sentences.

1. a. I am not shy. ✓
   b. I'm not shy.

2. a. It is typical to feel that way.
   b. It's typical to feel that way. ✓

3. a. He is not a teenager. He is an adult.
   b. He isn't a teenager. He's an adult. ✓

4. a. She is a child. She is six years old. ✓
   b. She's a child. She's six years old.

5. a. We are not only brothers. We are twins.
   b. We're not only brothers. We're twins. ✓

6. a. They are not my parents. They are my friends. ✓
   b. They aren't my parents. They're my friends. *what*

B Work with a partner. Take turns choosing either sentence *a* or sentence *b* from exercise A. Read your sentence aloud. Your partner says *sentence a* or *sentence b*.

C With your partner, take turns using *be* and the words in the box to make three sentences about you or your family. Use contractions.

> *I'm a teenager. I'm not an adult. My parents aren't in this country.*

teenager	years old	shy	parents	adult

EVERYDAY LANGUAGE Getting Someone's Attention

More Formal	**Less Formal**
Excuse me…	*Hi!*
Can I talk to you for a minute?	*Do you have a minute?*
Can I ask you a question?	*Marta?* (Say their name.)

D Walk around the classroom. Use the *Everyday Language* phrases to get someone's attention. Then ask them one of the questions below. After the first conversation, say goodbye and get someone else's attention. Ask each question at least once.

1. A: What country are you from? B: I'm from _____.
2. A: Are you a new student? B: No, I'm not. I started here _____ ago.
3. A: How do you like this weather? B: It's _____.

E Work with a new partner. Discuss how you get someone's attention in each situation. Then role play each situation. Choose your best situation and role play it for the class.

a teacher in class (You have a question about homework.)	**a waiter in a restaurant** (There is something wrong with your order.)
a friend in a store (You want an opinion about something you want to buy.)	**a stranger on the street** (You need directions to the train station.)

◀ Students try to get their teacher's attention. "Excuse me, Mr. Sarto. May I ask you a question?"

FINAL TASK Giving a Presentation about Yourself

> You will give a presentation about yourself and the things that are important in your life. You will create a pie chart and present it to the class.

A Work with a partner. Parents, family, friends, experiences, and media can change a teenager's ideas or actions. How do they change your ideas or actions? Give examples. Tell your partner.

PERSONALIZING

B Look at Jenna's pie chart. It shows how important each thing is in her life. What is important in your life? Make your own pie chart.

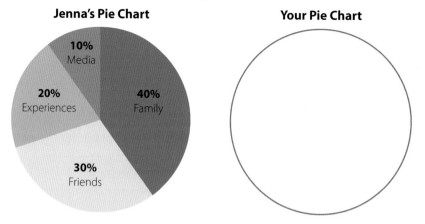

Jenna's Pie Chart

Your Pie Chart

C Read Jenna's presentation based on her pie chart in exercise B. Use Jenna's presentation as a model to help you write your own presentation (but use your pie chart).

> *Parents, family, friends, experiences, and the media all make us who we are. As you can see from my chart, my parents are the most important for me. They are kind people, and I am friendly because of them. My friends are also important in my life. I spend a lot of time with them. I learn a lot from my experiences when I travel, too. I don't watch a lot of TV or surf the Internet much, so the media doesn't really change my ideas or actions.*

PRESENTATION SKILL Making Eye Contact

Looking at your audience is very important. Making eye contact shows that you are interested in them. They will listen more closely. Follow these tips:

- Look at the audience's faces (the tops of the heads may be easier at first).
- Look around the audience (not at just one person or one side of the room).

D Practice your presentation with a partner. Remember to make eye contact.

E Give your presentation to the class. Remember to look around the audience. Show your pie chart to the class as you speak.

REFLECTION

1. How does thinking about your prior knowledge help you in class and outside of class?

   _____

   _____

2. How are you the same as and different from other people from your country? Give examples of each.

   _____

   _____

3. Here are the vocabulary words from the unit. Check (✓) the ones you can use.

   ☐ adult AWL   ☐ kind (n)   ☐ typical
   ☐ change   ☐ music   ☐ the world
   ☐ favorite   ☐ parents   ☐ years old
   ☐ friendly   ☐ science   ☐ vacation
   ☐ grow up   ☐ shy
   ☐ hobby   ☐ teenager

LOVE YOUR JOB 2

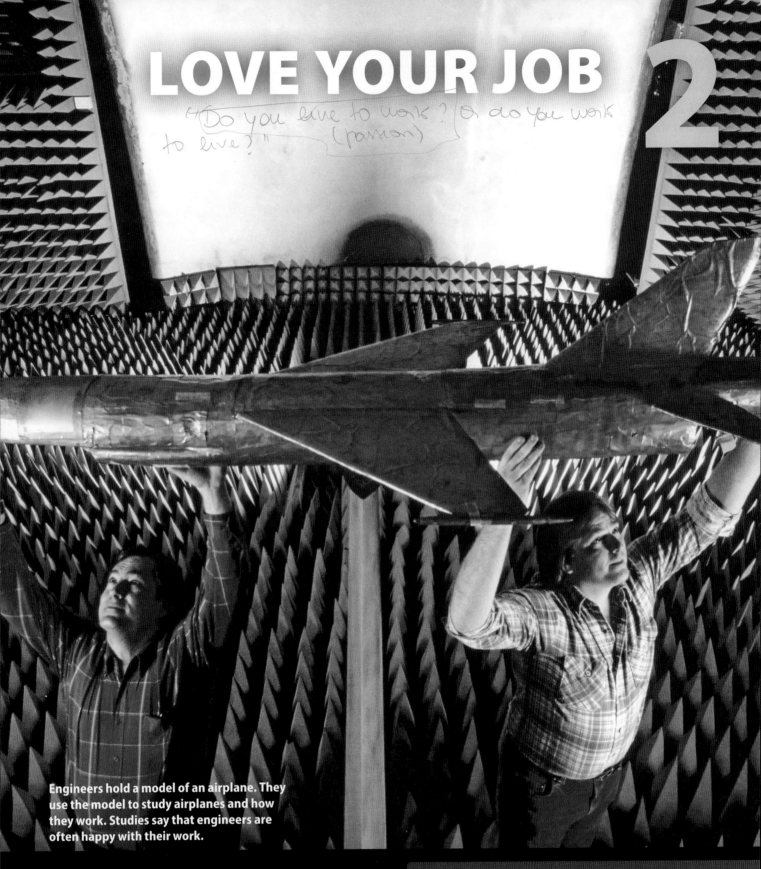

"Do you live to work? Or do you work to live?" (passion)

Engineers hold a model of an airplane. They use the model to study airplanes and how they work. Studies say that engineers are often happy with their work.

ACADEMIC SKILLS

LISTENING	Listening for Signposts
	Making a List
SPEAKING	Using Listing Words
	Simple Present -s Form of a Verb
CRITICAL THINKING	Categorizing Information

THINK AND DISCUSS

1 What do the men in the photo do? (What is their job?)
2 What subjects do people in this job need to study in school?
3 Do you want a job like this? Explain your answer.

Look at the photo and read the information. Then discuss the questions.

1. Describe the student in the photo. How does he feel? Why?

2. Look at the pie chart. Do you ever feel stress at work or school? Are your reasons the same as any in the chart? Tell which ones or any other reasons you have.

3. Read the tips for beating stress. Do you do any of these things? Which do you think are the best ideas? Explain.

BEATING STRESS

A student takes a nap during his lunch break in Anhui Province, China. The National College Entrance Exam, or the "Gao Kao," is given in June every year and is very stressful.

STRESS AT WORK:

WHY WE HAVE IT & HOW TO BEAT IT

Pie chart or Pie graphic

Beating = fighting

6%
Afraid to fail or lose job

20%
Work vs. private/family life

46%
Too much work

28%
Problems with people at work

How can you beat stress?

Experts say to try the following.

1. Don't eat sugar or other foods that cause more stress.

2. Get out of your chair and walk around.

3. Listen to music.

4. Do only one thing at a time.

5. Take deep breaths often.

6. Sleep seven or more hours a night.

Beat it! = get out! = go planning

A Vocabulary

A 🎧 1.16 Listen and check (✓) the words you already know.

☐ boring *(adj)*   ☐ create *(v)*   ☐ satisfied *(adj)*   ☐ try *(v)*
☐ boss *(n)*   ☐ exciting *(adj)*   ☐ together *(adv)*   ☐ work *(n)*

MEANING FROM
CONTEXT

B 🎧 1.17 Look at the chart and listen to information about people and their jobs. Then read the summary below. Notice each word in **blue** and think about its meaning.

[handwritten notes in margin]
Bar Graph
1) title
2) Axis
 horizontal axis
 ↳ describing jobs feelings
Vertical axis
percentage
counting by 20's.
"all in all"
= in total
in conclusion

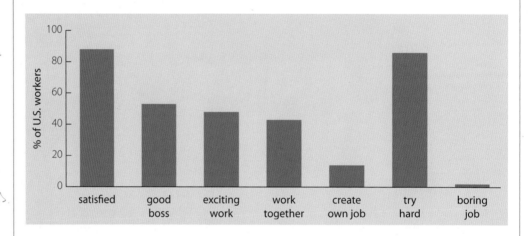

HOW U.S. WORKERS FEEL ABOUT THEIR JOBS *(Title)*

[bar chart: y-axis "% of U.S. workers" from 0 to 100; x-axis categories: satisfied, good boss, exciting work, work together, create own job, try hard, boring job]

88 percent of U.S. workers are **satisfied** with their job. They are happy in their **work**.

53 percent of workers think a good **boss** is important.

48 percent of workers think their work is **exciting**.

43 percent of workers think that working **together** with other people is important.

14 percent of workers **create** their own job.

86 percent of workers **try** hard at their job.

2 percent of people think their job is **boring**.

▶ **Dr. Alan Guth, a theoretical physicist who seems to enjoy his work**

[handwritten note: Bouajar = yawn.]

C Write the correct word from exercise A next to its definition.

1. ___Work___ job = occupation = carrier
2. ___Satisfied___ feeling happy
3. ___Exciting___ very interesting
4. ___boss___ the person you work for
5. ___together___ with another person or people
6. ___Boring___ not interesting
7. ___Try___ to make an effort to do something   effort = try
8. ___Create___ to make

VOCABULARY SKILL Antonyms

An antonym is a word that is the opposite of another word.

Word	Antonym
good	bad
adult	child

Knowing the antonym of a word can help you understand meanings of words. Start making an antonym list in your vocabulary notebook to help increase your vocabulary.

D Complete the chart with the antonyms of these words from exercise A. Use a dictionary if necessary. Then think of another word and write it and the antonym in the chart. Share your word with a partner. Write your partner's word in the chart, too.

Word	Antonym
boring	Exciting
together	alone
satisfied	disatisfied / disappointed

E Discuss the questions with a small group.

1. What is most important to you for your work? Friendly people? A good boss?
2. Tell about the type of boss you want to have.
3. Do you like to work together with other people or do you prefer to work alone?

Listening Online Lecture: Who's happy at work?

BEFORE LISTENING

PRIOR KNOWLEDGE **A** What do you think is important to be happy at work? Choose your top three things. Then compare your answers with a partner.

☒ money   ☒ exciting work   ☒ a good boss
☐ friendly people   ☐ creating things   ☐ helping others

WHILE LISTENING

LISTENING FOR MAIN IDEAS **B** 🎧 1.18 ▶ 1.3 Listen to the lecture. What is the main idea? Check (✓) the correct answer.

1. _____ choosing the best job

2. ☒ what makes people happy at work

3. _____ the world's happiest jobs

4. ✓ how to be happy at work

(handwritten notes in margin: good Boss · gratitude · appreciation · thankful)

C 🎧 1.18 Choose T for *True* or F for *False*. Listen again if necessary.

1. Many people say that money is the most important thing in a job.   T   **F**

2. Many people look for a job that helps other people.   **T**   F

3. Many people are happy when they can create things.   **T**   F

4. Many people don't want to work with other people.   T   **F**

5. Not many teachers like their jobs.   T   **F**

(handwritten note: cub = baby)

▶ A keeper puts giant panda cub Qi Yi on a bed at Chengdu Research Base in Chengdu, China.

(handwritten notes in margin: Happy coworkers work hard + like jobs + friendly = good work environment)

Signposts = transition words.

LISTENING SKILL Listening for Signposts

When speakers list something, they usually use signpost words. These words and phrases tell the listener there will be a new idea. Some specific signpost words and phrases to listen for are:

First… Second… Third…

One reason… Another point…

Also…

The last thing…

D 🎧 1.19 Listen for the signposts in the excerpt from the lecture. Notice the information after each signpost. Complete it with the words you hear.

1. One thing that many people look for: a job that *helps other people*.

2. Another thing people want from a job is to *create things*.

3. Also, people want their boss to *thank you them*.

4. Finally, people want to have *happy co-workers*.

E 🎧 1.20 Listen to the excerpts from the lecture. Answer the questions.

LISTENING FOR DETAILS

1. According to the lecturer, which jobs are two of the happiest jobs?

   Engen   *Teachers*

2. Happiness is one thing people look for in a job. What are two other things?

   Help other people   *a boss that thanks them*
   happy co-workers   *create things.*

AFTER LISTENING

F Think about a job you have or had. Check (✓) the good things about the job and add two more good (or bad) things. Then tell a small group about the job. Use signposts.

PERSONALIZING

Job: *Account*

☐ help people

☒ money

☒ boss thanks you

☐ happy co-workers

☐ create something new

☒ good location (where you work)

☒ *English communication*

☐ _____

A Speaking

GRAMMAR FOR SPEAKING Simple Present

Use the simple present to talk about:

- facts or truths. (An *engineer* **creates** things. Teachers **help** people.)
- schedules or routines. (*They* **work** every Saturday. My work **begins** at 9:00 a.m.)
- habits or repeated events. (*They* **try** hard at work. My boss **says** thank you every day.)

Affirmative	Negative
I/You/We/They **work**.	*We* **don't work**.
He/She/It **works**.	*He/She/It* **doesn't work**.

Yes/No Questions	Answers
Do you **work**?	*Yes,* I **do**. / *No,* I **don't**.
Does she **work**?	*Yes, she* **does**. / *No, she* **doesn't**.

A Take notes in the chart about a job you want to have in the future. Write the job and one or more skills needed for the job. Then, with a partner, interview each other about the job. Use the conversation below.

Job	Duties

A: Do you work?
B: Yes, I do. / No, I don't.
A: What do you do? / What kind of job do you want?
B: I'm a _Account_____. / I want to be a
   _____.
A: What does a _____ do?
B: _____

B Tell the class about your partner's job or future job.

> *My partner, Pierre, wants to be a chef. He loves cooking. A chef knows about different kinds of foods and cooks food for a lot of people.*

C Choose the correct verb to complete the sentence.

1. A web designer (need / needs) a lot of experience.
2. Teachers (help / helps) people learn new things.
3. A photographer (take / takes) a lot of photos.
4. A server (bring / brings) people food at a restaurant.
5. Engineers (create / creates) different products.

D With a partner, discuss what is good and bad about each job in exercise C.

> *A server helps people enjoy their meal. A server doesn't get a lot of money.*

tongue twister.

PRONUNCIATION Simple Present -s Form of the Verb

🎧 1.21 The -s/-es at the end of a verb after *he/she/it* has three possible sounds: /s/, /z/, and /əz/ (or /ɪz/).

The -s/-es sounds like:

voiceless
voiced
sibilant

• /s/ after verbs ending in /f, k, p, t/.	*laughs, works, keeps, meets*
• /z/ after verbs ending in /b, d, g, l, m, n, ŋ, r, v/ and all vowel sounds.	*needs, calls, begins, moves, sees, goes*
• /əz/ after verbs ending in /s, ʃ, tʃ, z, dʒ/.	*misses, mixes, pushes, teaches, uses, judges*

ŋ = ng (strong) (going)

Note: Only the /əz/ (or /ɪz/) makes a separate syllable: *tea-ches.*

E 🎧 1.22 Listen for the /s/, /z/, or /əz/ at the end of each verb. Check (✓) the sound you hear. Then practice saying each word.

	/s/	/z/	/əz/
1. creates	☒	☐	☐
2. reads	☐	☒	☐
3. fixes	☐	☐	☒
4. gives	☐	☒	☐
5. knows	☐	☒	☐
6. washes	☐	☐	☒
7. helps	☒	☐	☐
8. tries	☐	☒	☐
9. catches	☐	☐	☒
10. sits	☒	☐	☐

F 🎧 1.23 Listen to Allissa and check (✓) the things she often does for her job.

☐ call	☒ talk to customers	☐ use a computer	☒ show	☐ create
☒ explain	☐ teach	☒ learn	☐ sell	☒ help

G With a partner, take turns asking and answering questions about Allissa from exercise F. Use the model conversation below. Be sure to say the final -s correctly.

A: *Does Allissa <u>talk to customers</u>?*

B: *Yes, she <u>talks to customers</u> all day.*

H What do you think Allissa's job is? Tell your class your ideas.

CRITICAL THINKING:
CATEGORIZING

I Work with a partner. What does a person in each job in the chart do every day?
Discuss your answers and complete the chart using the phrases in the box. Use the -s
form of the verbs.

> *A salesperson sells products.*

talk with people	~~teach~~	~~call customers~~	~~use a computer~~
create activities	~~create products~~	~~sell products~~	~~create web pages~~
work with others	~~write~~	~~explain~~	~~work alone~~

Web Designer	Salesperson	Engineer	Teacher
create web pages *use computer* *work alone*	*sells products* *call customers*	*create products*	*teaches* *explain* *write* *create activities*

**A teacher explains an
activity to students
in a classroom in
Chickmagalur, India.**

LESSON TASK Discussing Different Types of Jobs

A Look at the jobs in the box. Check (✓) the jobs that you know. Use a dictionary to look up any words you don't know.

- ☑ architect
- ☑ computer programmer
- ☑ doctor
- ☑ hairstylist
- ☑ lawyer
- ☑ pilot
- ☑ receptionist
- ☑ writer
- ☑ veterinarian

B Categorize the jobs from exercise A in the chart. Some jobs can go in more than one category.

CRITICAL THINKING: CATEGORIZING

Creative	Boring	Exciting	Well-paid
Architect Hairstylist comp. programmer	Receptionist veterinarian	Writer pilot	Lawyer Doctor pilot

C Work with a partner and compare your charts. Explain why you categorized the jobs the way you did.

PERSONALIZING

> *I put <u>veterinarian</u> in the "well-paid" category because <u>vets make a lot of money</u>. Which category did you put <u>pilot</u> in?* I put pilot in the "Exciting" category because pilot travel around the world.

D What job is good for you? Tell your partner and explain why.

> *I think a <u>veterinarian</u> is a good job for me. I love animals, and cats and dogs always like me. I also want to make money!*

E Take turns telling your class about your partner. Tell your class if you agree.

> *Takahashi wants to be a <u>veterinarian</u>. He loves animals, and cats and dogs always like him. He also wants to make money! I think this is a good job for him. He's very kind and seems friendly.*

F Work in a small group. Read the quote and discuss its meaning. Then share your answers with the class.

CRITICAL THINKING: INTERPRETING

"If you do a job you love, you will never work a day in your life."

Video

Wanted: Adventure Storyteller

Adventure storyteller Fitz Cahall interviews mountain climber Kyle Dempster.

BEFORE VIEWING

A Read the information about Fitz Cahall. With a partner, discuss what you think an "adventure storyteller" is.

> **FITZ CAHALL** is a filmmaker, a photographer, and an adventure storyteller. He makes films and writes blogs about National Geographic's Adventurers of the Year. He tells their stories.

PRIOR KNOWLEDGE **B** Work with a partner. How do people usually get a job? Discuss and list some ways.

They hear about it from a friend.   Social Media (Lim)

        Networking

C Match each word from the video with its meaning. Use your dictionary to help you.

1. _f_ hire   a. something you want to do
2. _d_ job description   b. possible danger
3. _e_ give up   c. help you be happy or to work well (passion)
4. _a_ dream BIG   d. a list of the skills needed to do a job
5. _c_ make you tick —what's   e. to stop trying
   your passion'
6. _b_ risk   f. to give someone a job

WHILE VIEWING

D ▶ **1.4** Watch the video. Then choose the correct answers.

UNDERSTANDING MAIN IDEAS

1. How did Cahall get his job as an adventure storyteller?
   a. National Geographic hired him.
   b. *(circled)* He created his own job.
   c. People hired him to write about their stories.
   d. He doesn't have a job.

2. What does Cahall think about work?
   a. Create your own job.
   b. Get a lot of money.
   c. Work is boring.
   d. *(circled)* Do what you love.

3. Once he created his own job, what did he do?
   a. *(circled)* He started a radio show and made films.
   b. He became famous.
   c. He had a son.
   d. He got a boring job.

4. What is one thing Cahall wants to do?
   a. be an Adventurer of the Year
   b. have a normal job in an office
   c. *(circled)* spend a lot of time outside
   d. take up skydiving as a new hobby

5. How many stories did Cahall write?
   a. 5   b. *(circled)* 10   c. 15   d. 20

E ▶ **1.4** Watch the video again. Complete the sentences with the information you hear.

UNDERSTANDING DETAILS

1. There wasn't really a __job description__ for what I wanted to do.

2. People don't __hire__ storytellers…

3. That was my __dream__.

4. Nobody was going to give me this job. I had to go __create__ it. *= make happen.*

5. There are a lot of ways to take __risks__ in life.

6. You have to do the thing that __makes you tick__.

AFTER VIEWING

F Discuss the questions with a partner or in a small group.

CRITICAL THINKING: REFLECTING

1. Cahall says that you should do the thing that "makes you tick." What are the things that make Cahall tick?

2. What makes you tick? Give examples of work you love to do and work you don't enjoy doing. Explain. *PASSION. / Motivation /*

- get promotion my job

I make me tick is improving my English communication.

Vocabulary

A 🎧 1.24 Listen and check (✓) the words you already know. Then discuss their meaning with a partner. Check the dictionary for any you are not sure about.

☐ advice *(n)* ☐ contacts *(n)* ☐ fail *(v)* ☐ own *(adj)*
☐ company *(n)* ☐ enjoy *(v)* ☐ manager *(n)* ☐ skills *(n)*

MEANING FROM
CONTEXT

B 🎧 1.25 Complete the paragraph with a word from exercise A. Then listen and check your answers.

[handwritten: Traih ≠ skills]

CAREER ADVICE FROM AN ARTIST

I always say: *Life is short, so love what you do.* You should *always* __enjoy__ (1) your work. Here's some great __advice__ (2) someone gave me when I was young.

First, think about what you are good at and use the __skills__ (3) you already have. Are you good with people? Are you creative? Do you want to be a __manager__ (4) or a supervisor? Or do you want to be the boss and maybe have your __boss__ (5) business some day? I started my __company__ (6) when I was just 25. It was scary, but also exciting!

Second, when you begin to look for a job, start with your family and friends. These __contacts__ (7) can help you find a job. As they say, it's not *what* you know, but *who* you know. *[handwritten: → networking]*

Finally, remember that you may __fail__ (8) at first, but don't quit. Keep trying, again and again, to do what you love!

▼ **Brazilian artist Mundano works on a mural in Rio de Janeiro, Brazil.**

C Read the sentences. Notice the underlined word or phrase. Match it with the word or phrase with the same meaning.

1. __d__ Think about the <u>skills you have</u>.

2. __f__ Talk to all of <u>your contacts</u> when you are looking for a job.

3. __e__ It's important to do what you <u>enjoy</u>.

4. __a__ Some people <u>fail</u> at first.

5. __g__ Do you want to have <u>your own company</u>?

6. __b__ The best <u>managers</u> are good with people.

7. __c__ Some good <u>advice</u> is to never give up.

a. don't do well

b. bosses and supervisors

c. ideas from other people

d. things you are good at

e. like

f. the people you know

g. a business that is yours

D Work with a partner. Discuss these questions.

1. When you are looking for a job, what types of people can you use as contacts? Write several possible contacts (e.g., teachers, ...) in your notebook.

2. Do you agree with the advice in exercise B? Explain.

3. What are some pros (good things) and cons (bad things) of being a manager? Write your answers in the chart.

Pros + good things	Cons + bad things

Listening An Interview about 21st Century Jobs

BEFORE LISTENING

PREDICTING **A** Work with a partner. Look at the list of 21st century jobs. What do you think people with these jobs do? Tell your partner. Make a prediction if don't know for sure.

app designer / developer   life coach   sleep coach
cloud services specialist   playlist professional   social media manager

WHILE LISTENING

LISTENING FOR **B** 🎧 1.26 Listen to the conversation. Check (✓) the three main ideas.
MAIN IDEAS

1. _____ We live in a computer age.

2. _____ People can create their own jobs now.

3. _____ The digital age provides opportunities for new jobs.

4. _____ There are a lot of new apps.

5. _____ Social media managers and bloggers show and sell products for companies.

6. _____ People are creative and find out what people need.

C 🎧 1.27 Listen to the excerpt from the conversation and complete the sentences with the words you hear.

1. People _____ new jobs each year.

2. These are _____ we didn't have five or ten years ago.

3. One, we live in the _____ age, and things are _____ every year. And two, people are _____ .

▼ Young business people working in creative room spaces at a modern startup office

One way to take notes as you listen is to make a list. A list helps you organize the information you hear. Numbering the points in the list helps keep the different ideas organized.

D 🎧 1.28 Listen for the advice that Natalia Stewart gives. Make a list of the items.

NOTE TAKING

1. _____

2. _____

3. _____

4. _____

E 🎧 1.29 Listen to the excerpt from the conversation. Match the job to its description.

LISTENING FOR DETAILS

1. _____ sleep coach

a. teaches people how to be satisfied and happy

2. _____ life coach

b. creates lists of songs for companies

3. _____ playlist professional

c. manages the things people keep on the Internet

4. _____ cloud specialist

d. helps people to rest at night

AFTER LISTENING

F Work in a small group. Discuss these questions.

1. What is some other advice you know for getting a job?
2. Which of the new jobs from the conversation sound interesting or exciting to you? Which sound boring? Explain.

G Work with a partner. Discuss the pros (good things) and cons (bad things) of creating your own job. Write your ideas in the chart.

CRITICAL THINKING: ANALYZING

Pros	Cons

B | Speaking

CRITICAL THINKING:
SYNTHESIZING

A Look at the photos and read the information. Discuss the questions in a small group.

1. What do these people have in common?
2. What can we learn about failing from them?

▷ **(Left) Walt Disney tried 302 times to get money from a bank to help him start Disneyland.**

▷ **(Right) J. K. Rowling tried to sell her first book in the Harry Potter series to 12 different companies.**

▷ **Thomas Edison failed thousands of times before he invented the lightbulb.**

SPEAKING SKILL Using Listing Words

In lesson A, you practiced listening for signpost words and phrases speakers use to organize their ideas. Using listing words is one way to organize your ideas as you speak.

Some listing words include:

First… Second… Third… (First, I like to work with people.)
One… Two… Three… (There are a few reasons. One, we live in the computer age.)

B Why is failing good for people? Write your ideas in the first column. Then take turns sharing your ideas with a partner. Use listing words. Write your partner's ideas in the second column.

My Ideas	My Partner's Ideas

C With a partner, discuss these questions. Remember to show interest when the other person is talking.

1. What do you do when you fail at something?

2. If something is difficult, do you give up easily?

3. Do you try again when you fail?

4. Is it ever OK to give up?

for Monday

FINAL TASK Presenting your Dream Job

You will give a one-minute presentation about your dream job. First, you'll brainstorm your skills. Next you'll think about the types of activities you enjoy. Then you'll write and practice your presentation.

A Write questions to help your partner decide what he or she is good at. Take turns asking and answering the questions. Take notes and think about your partner's skills. Then give your partner suggestions.

CRITICAL THINKING: ANALYZING

Questions	My Partner's Answers
What is your favorite school subject? Why?	

B What kinds of activities do you enjoy doing? Check (✓) the types of activities you enjoy.

_____ Writing (Jobs: secretary, assistant)

_____ Working on the computer (Jobs: computer programmer, social media specialist)

_____ Talking to people (Jobs: salesperson, nurse, teacher)

_____ Working outside (Jobs: forest ranger, mail carrier)

_____ Working with your hands (Jobs: mechanic, engineer)

_____ Being creative or artistic (Jobs: artist, singer, musician)

C Choose or create a job that is good for the skills you have and the kind of work you enjoy. Complete the chart. List the reasons why you are a good person for this job.

Job	
Reasons	1. _____
	2. _____
	3. _____

PRESENTATION SKILL Closing a Presentation

At the end of your presentation, it is good to signal that you are coming to the end. This helps your audience listen for the final points in your presentation. Here are some phrases you can use:

> To conclude, …
> In short, …
> In conclusion, …

D Read this short presentation. Use it to write your presentation, but add more details to yours. Remember to use listing words and a closing phrase.

> > My dream job is to be a dog trainer. First, I am very good with dogs. I know how to work with dogs, and they work well with me, too. Second, I like to work outside. Dog trainers work outside a lot. Third, I am good with people. Dog trainers talk to people about their dogs. In conclusion, my dream job is to be a dog trainer.

E Work with a partner and practice giving your presentation. Give each other ideas on how to make the presentation better.

F Give your presentation to the class.

REFLECTION

1. What are some words and phrases you can use to list reasons when speaking?

   _____
   _____

2. Which topic from the unit will help you think more about your own career? Explain.

   _____
   _____

3. Here are the vocabulary words from the unit. Check (✔) the ones you can use.

   ☐ advice   ☐ enjoy   ☐ skills
   ☐ boring   ☐ exciting   ☐ together
   ☐ boss   ☐ fail   ☐ try
   ☐ company   ☐ manager   ☐ work
   ☐ contact ᴬᵂᴸ   ☐ own
   ☐ create ᴬᵂᴸ   ☐ satisfied

UNUSUAL DESTINATIONS 3

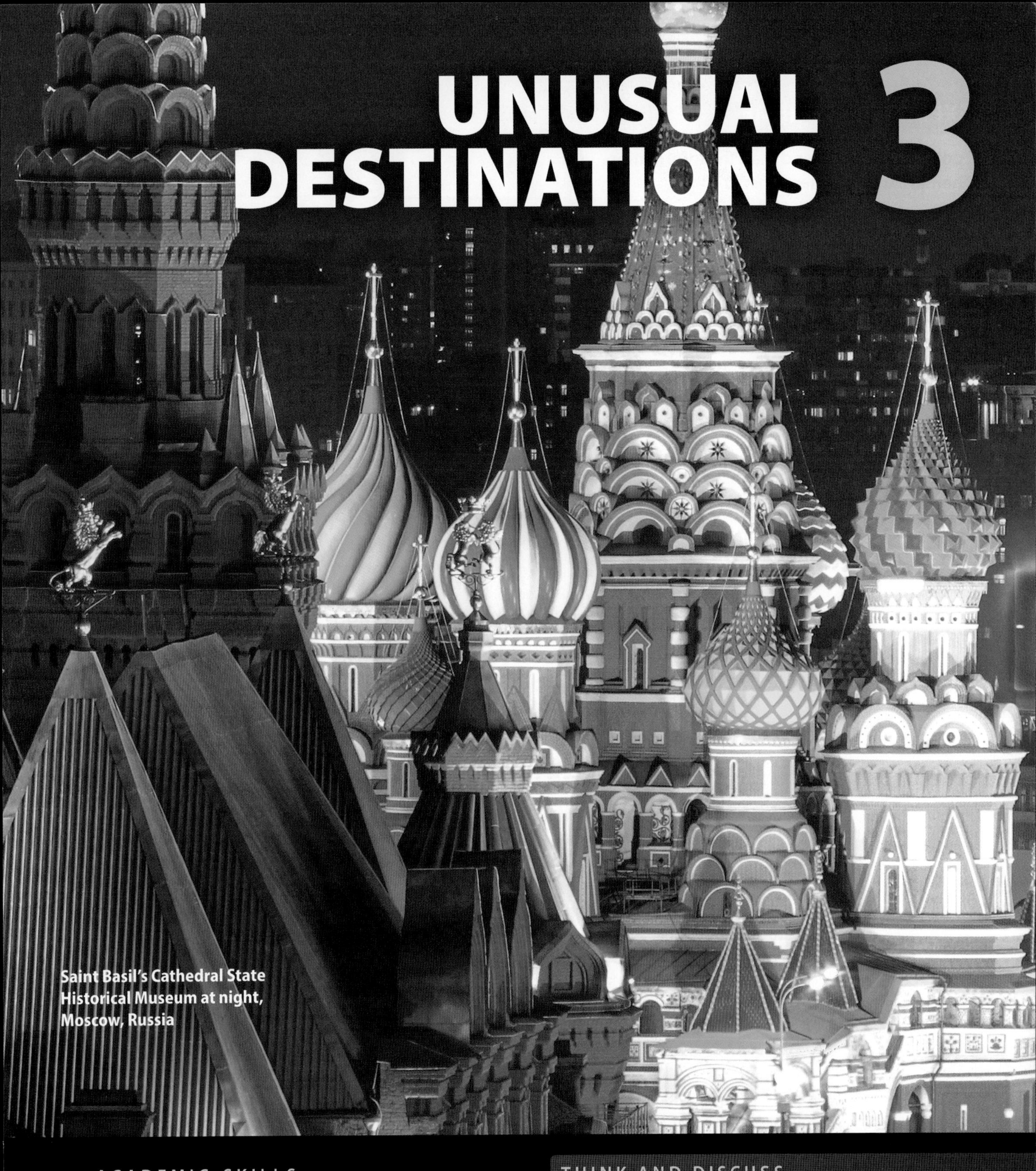

Saint Basil's Cathedral State Historical Museum at night, Moscow, Russia

ACADEMIC SKILLS

LISTENING Listening for Details
Using a *Wh-* Question Chart

SPEAKING Agreeing and Disagreeing
Syllables and Stress

CRITICAL THINKING Thinking about Pros and Cons

THINK AND DISCUSS

1 What is this a photo of? What time of day is it?
2 Does this look like other places you've seen? How is it different?
3 Are you interested in visiting Russia? Explain.

Look at the photos and read the information. Then discuss the questions.

1. Which place in the photos do you most want to visit? Explain.

2. Do you prefer to visit cities or more natural places for vacation? Explain.

3. Tell about an interesting place you visited.

LET'S TAKE A TRIP!

At night, visitors look at one of many beautiful buildings in the ancient city of Petra, Jordan.

Guests enjoy a dinner party in an underwater tunnel at the Tianjin Haichang Polar Ocean World in Tianjin, China.

Late fall and winter are great times to see the beautiful aurora borealis (northern lights). Visitors stay in teepees in Aurora Village, Northwest Territories, Canada.

A Vocabulary

A 🎧 **1.30** Listen and check (✓) the words you already know. Then discuss their meaning with a partner. Check the dictionary for any you are not sure about.

□ area (n)   □ crowded (adj)   □ quiet (adj) *= silent*   □ unusual (adj)
□ beautiful (adj)   □ famous (adj)   □ tourists (n)   □ visit (v)

MEANING FROM CONTEXT

B 🎧 **1.31** Complete Fatima and Arturo's conversation with a word from exercise A. Then listen and check your answers.

HOW ABOUT EQI GLACIER?

Fatima: Hi, Arturo. I'm trying to plan my summer vacation. Should I go to the beach, like I always do? Or should I try a __famous__ place, like Paris? Or maybe a new and very
                                          1
different destination—somewhere __unusual__ ? What do you think?
                                        2

Arturo: I think you should try somewhere unusual! I saw a TV show about an amazing glacier in Greenland. It's called Eqi Glacier. The ice on the glacier is so clear, and the snow is very white. It's so __beautiful__ . Not many people go there, so it's not __crowded__ .
                        3   4

Fatima: Hmm… It sounds like a great place to __visit__ , especially in the hot
                                                    5
summer months! And I like that there aren't many __tourists__ there. I like to go to
                                                        6
__quiet__ places. In my opinion, the fewer people, the better!
      7   *comparative (#)*

Arturo: Well, it looks like a great __area__ where you can relax and have fun!
                                        8

**Tourists viewing the breathtaking
Eqi Glacier in Greenland**

C Write each word from exercise A next to its definition.

1. _quiet_ not loud
2. _area_ a part of a city or country ⇒ spot
3. _visit_ to go to a place
4. _unusual_ different
5. _beautiful_ very pretty
6. _crowed_ full of people
7. _famous_ well-known
8. _tourists_ a people who travel to a place for fun

VOCABULARY SKILL Synonyms

A synonym is a word that has a similar meaning to another word or phrase.

*Tourists go to that **area**. / Tourists go to that **spot**.*
*It was an **unusual** vacation. / It was a **different** vacation.*

Here are some tips to help you learn them:

- Pay attention to synonyms in both listening and reading.
- Write synonyms for words you already know in your vocabulary notebook.

D Write each word next to its synonym. Then add two or more synonyms. Use a dictionary.

peaceful	traveler	go to	pretty	full

1. visit _go to, see, stop by_
2. beautiful _pretty, wonderful, good looking, attractive, gorgeous_
3. quiet _peaceful, silent, mute_
4. crowded _full, "cramped like sardines" "cramped like a box of matches" congested_
5. tourist _traveler, visitors, Nomad, tripe, adventure._

E Complete the sentences with personal information. Then share your sentences with the class. Try to use words from exercise A and synonyms from exercise D.

PERSONALIZING

1. I want to visit a/an _unusual_ area because I _____.

2. A beautiful place to visit in my country is _____
   because _____.

3. A famous place to visit in my country is _____.
   It is _____.

Listening Presentation: Unusual Southeast Asia

BEFORE LISTENING

PRIOR KNOWLEDGE   **A**   Look at the map and the photos. What do you know about the countries in the photos? Tell a partner.

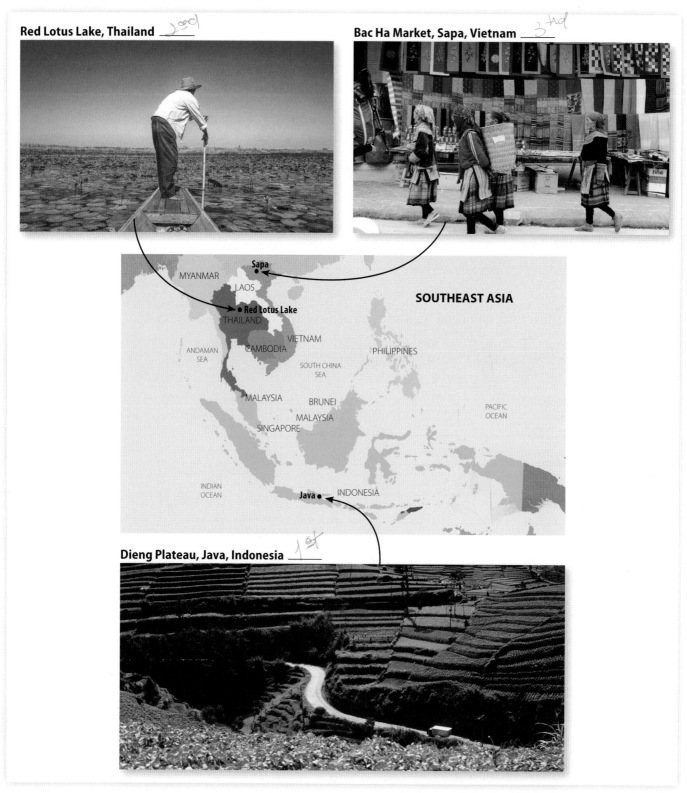

Red Lotus Lake, Thailand _2nd_

Bac Ha Market, Sapa, Vietnam _3rd_

SOUTHEAST ASIA

MYANMAR

Sapa

LAOS

● Red Lotus Lake

THAILAND

VIETNAM

ANDAMAN SEA

CAMBODIA

PHILIPPINES

SOUTH CHINA SEA

MALAYSIA

BRUNEI

MALAYSIA

SINGAPORE

PACIFIC OCEAN

INDIAN OCEAN

Java ●

INDONESIA

Dieng Plateau, Java, Indonesia _1st_

B Look at the map and read the statements. Choose **T** for *True* or **F** for *False*.

CRITICAL THINKING: ANALYZING VISUALS

1. Indonesia is north of Thailand.   T **(F)**

2. Java is in Indonesia.   **(T)** F

3. Thailand is an island.   T **(F)**

4. Thailand and Vietnam are next to each other. **(T)** F

5. Singapore is south of Vietnam.   **(T)** F

6. Vietnam is on the South China Sea.   **(T)** F

WHILE LISTENING

C 🎧 1.32 ▶ 1.5 Listen and check (✓) the two main ideas about the presentation.

LISTENING FOR MAIN IDEAS

1. _____ Susana Jenkins writes blogs.

2. _✓_ Unusual places are great to travel to.

3. _____ Susana Jenkins does not enjoy crowded places.

4. _✓_ Southeast Asia has a variety of unusual places.

5. _____ Big cities have many beautiful temples and palaces.

D 🎧 1.33 Look at the photos in exercise A and listen to an excerpt from the presentation. Above each photo, number the places the speaker talks about first, second, and third.

> **LISTENING SKILL** Listening for Details
>
> Speakers give details to explain or support their main ideas. Details are facts, stories, numbers, lists, reasons, examples, or other pieces of information. Listening for and noting the important details help you learn and remember information.

E 🎧 1.33 Listen to the excerpt again. Match the place with the detail the speaker gives about it.

LISTENING FOR DETAILS

1. Dieng Plateau, Java, Indonesia _c_   a. away from the beaches

2. Red Lotus Lake, Thailand _a_   b. lively and colorful

3. Bac Ha Market, Sapa, Vietnam _b_   c. like steps in the mountains

AFTER LISTENING

F Work in a small group. Discuss the questions.

CRITICAL THINKING: SYNTHESIZING

1. Which book do you think Susana Jenkins wrote? Explain.

   - *Most Famous Places to Visit*
   - *A Different Kind of Trip*
   - *Ten Tours to Take Before You Turn 50!*

2. Which of the three places on page 46 do you want to visit the most? Explain.

Speaking

SPEAKING SKILL Agreeing and Disagreeing

Agreeing: Use these expressions to agree with someone.

A: *I like to travel.*
B: ***I do, too. / Me, too!***

A: *I don't like to be a tourist.*
B: ***I don't, either. / Me, neither.***

Disagreeing: When disagreeing, it's important to be polite. Say, *Oh, really?* or *That's interesting!* or another phrase before you disagree.

A: *I like to go on long walks on vacation.*
B: ***That's interesting. I don't.*** *I prefer to lie on the beach.*

A: *I don't like to travel in a group.*
B: ***Oh really? I do!*** *I love it.*

A 🎧 1.34 Listen to the conversations. Do the speakers agree or disagree? Choose the correct answer. Then listen again and write the expression you hear.

1. ~~Agree~~ / Disagree   *That's Intrusting! I don't.*
2. Agree / ~~Disagree~~   *I don't, either*
3. ~~Agree~~ / Disagree   *Me, too!*
4. ~~Agree~~ / Disagree   *I do!*
5. ~~Agree~~ / Disagree   *I do too!*

B Write a sentence about the type of vacation you like. Then walk around the classroom and say your sentence to your classmates. Take note of how many students agree or disagree with you. Share your results with the class.

Sentence: _____

Agree: _____   Disagree: _____

Giza Pyramids, Egypt

Use the present continuous:

- to talk about things that are happening right now.
  I **am reading** now.

- to talk about activities that are ongoing over a period of time.
  He **is staying** at the beach all summer.

Affirmative

I**'m enjoying** my trip.
She**'s eating** at the hotel.
They**'re trying** a new place.

Negative

I**'m not taking** the tour.
She**'s not eating** local food.
They**'re not eating** at the hotel.

Yes/No Questions

Are you **working** next week?
Is she **learning** the language?

Answers

Yes, I **am**. / No, I**'m not**.
Yes, she **is**. / No, she **isn't**.

C 🎧 1.35 Complete the conversation with the present continuous form of the verbs in parentheses. Listen and repeat to check your answers.

A: Hi. What are you doing?

B: I _____ (look) at my photos from Egypt.
   ₁

A: What are you doing in this photo?

B: Oh, I _____ (ride) on a camel. In this photo, my friends and I
   ₂
   _____ (walk) on the beach.
   ₃

A: It's beautiful! What about this photo?

B: My friend _____ (drive) a motorcycle through Cairo.
   ₄

A: Wow! Sounds exciting!

B: Yes, at times. Oh, in this photo, my friends and I _____ (walk)
   ₅
   up the pyramids. And here is a photo of all of us. We _____
   ₆
   (rest) halfway up.

A: Funny! Well, at least you _____ (smile).
   ₇

D Work in a small group. Think about a photo of you on a vacation. Tell your classmates what you are doing on your vacation. Use some of the descriptive words in the box. Your classmates guess where you are.

A: *I'm walking. It's very hot. I'm smiling. The water is running around my toes.*

B: *You are at the beach!*

A: *Yes!*

hot	unusual	quiet	amazing
famous	crowded	dangerous	exciting

CRITICAL THINKING   Thinking about Pros and Cons

When we discuss topics and make decisions about things, it is helpful to think about the pros (good things) and the cons (bad things). Thinking about the pros and cons can help you make a decision or form your opinion.

E Work with a partner. Think about the pros and cons of visiting a typical vacation place and visiting an unusual place for vacation. Write your notes in the charts.

Typical Place	
Pros	**Cons**

Unusual Place	
Pros	**Cons**

F Form a group of four with another pair. Share your pros and cons lists. Discuss which type of place you want to go to on your next vacation.

LESSON TASK Planning a Vacation for your Teacher

A Look at these unusual destinations with a partner. Use words from the box to describe each place. Then write each word in the chart below. Add other words that you think describe these places.

CRITICAL THINKING: ANALYZING

exciting	cold	fun	famous
quiet	boring	crowded	beautiful

Snowboarding in Utah, USA

Cruise in Antarctica

Kayaking in the Philippines

Utah, USA	Antarctica	Philippines

B Work with your partner to discuss which vacation is best for your teacher. Remember to use the agreeing and disagreeing phrases from page 48 when deciding which vacation is best. Use the sample conversation as a guide.

A: I think our teacher wants to go to _____.

B: Why?

A: Because she/he _____.

C Share the vacation you chose for your teacher with the class. Explain why you think this vacation is best for him/her. After all classmates share their ideas, the teacher will tell you which vacation he/she prefers.

PRESENTING

Video

Monkey City

BEFORE VIEWING

PREDICTING **A** You will watch a video about an unusual city in Thailand with a lot of monkeys. What do you think the monkeys do? Make a list of of your predictions.

imagine what happen in the future

✓	Things the Monkeys Will Do

B Match each word from the video with its definition. Use a dictionary to help you.

1. symbol ___e___
2. prosperity ___e___
3. festival ___a___
4. statue ___b___ *madura*
5. naughty ___d___

a. *(n)* a big party

b. *(n)* form of a person or other thing made from stone, wood, or metal

c. *(n)* a sign that means something (e.g., =, +, −)

d. *(adj)* behaving badly

e. *(n)* having money

WHILE VIEWING

C ▶ 1.6 Watch the video and check (✓) your predictions in exercise A.

CHECKING PREDICTIONS

D ▶ 1.6 Watch the video again and answer the questions.

1. What are the two goals of the monkey festival in Lopburi? Check (✓) the two goals.

_____ Feed the tourists

_____ Make the people of Lopburi happy

___✓___ Bring food to the monkeys

_____ Teach the monkeys how to behave

___✓___ Bring tourists to the city

2. What did the monkey take from the tourist? _his Glasses_

3. What two things do the statues get during the festival?

_____food_____ , _____water_____

E ▶ 1.6 Watch the video again without the sound. With a partner, tell what the monkeys are (and aren't) doing in the video.

> *They are eating.* They are playing. They are stealing. They are drinking water

AFTER VIEWING

F Work in a small group. Discuss the questions.

PERSONALIZING

1. Monkeys are a symbol of prosperity and good luck in Thailand. What are symbols of good luck and prosperity in your country? *Pyramids* *rabbit's foot*

   Four-leaf clover

2. Would you like to go to Lopburi for the monkey festival? Why or why not?

G Work with a partner. What are the pros and cons of bringing tourists to a city? Write your ideas in the chart. Then form a group of with another pair and discuss your ideas.

CRITICAL THINKING: ANALYZING

> *I think it's good to have tourists. Tourists bring money to our town.*

Bringing Tourists to a City	
Pros	**Cons**
bring money to town · Create more new jobs · Partys (festival) · More people know · culture is more popular	· Crowded people (dirty) · Unclean streets · Prices highly (more expensive) · more traffic Desorder

Vocabulary

B

A 🎧 1.36 Listen and check (✓) the words you already know.

☐ amazing *(adj)* ☐ manmade *(adj)* ☐ modern *(adj)* ☐ special *(adj)*
☐ island *(n)* ☐ mix *(n)* ☐ natural *(adj)* ☐ view *(n)*

MEANING FROM CONTEXT

B 🎧 1.37 Look at the photo. Then read and listen to the information. Notice each word in **blue** and think about its meaning.

A MANMADE WONDER

There are many beautiful places on Earth. Some are **natural**, like beaches or mountains, and others are **manmade** like tall buildings or parks. One unusual destination in Dubai has a good **mix** of both. It is a manmade **island** close to the coast, and it looks like a palm tree. The **view** of the island from an airplane is **amazing**! The hotel is very new and **modern** with everything you need or want while on vacation. This destination provides a good mix of nature, beauty, excitement, and relaxation. It is a very **special** and unusual vacation place.

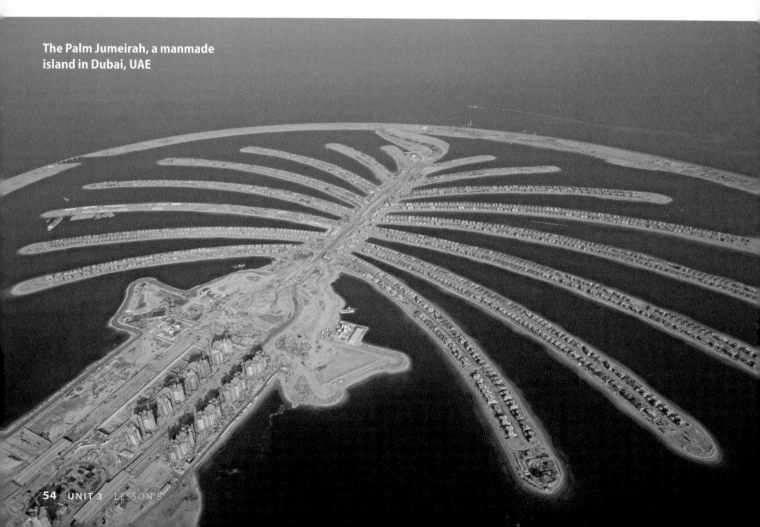

The Palm Jumeirah, a manmade island in Dubai, UAE

C Match each word from exercise A with its definition.

1. _e_ natural
2. _f_ manmade (human made)
3. _a_ special Unique
4. _h_ island
5. _d_ amazing
6. _c_ view
7. _b_ mix
8. _g_ modern

a. better or different (Unique)
b. two or more different things together
c. the area that you can see
d. very exciting or beautiful
e. something that people did not create
f. something that people created
g. new
h. land with water all around it

D With a partner, discuss these questions.

PERSONALIZING

1. Do you like natural or manmade places better?
2. Describe an amazing view in your city or country.

E Work in a group. Discuss natural and manmade places in your city, in your country, and around the world. Complete the chart. Then share the places with the rest of the class.

CRITICAL THINKING: CATEGORIZING

	City	Country	World
Natural			
Manmade			

F Have you ever visited one of the places in the chart? Was it a good place to visit? Why or why not?

> *I went to the Grand Canyon. The view was amazing.*

Listening   A Conversation about a Vacation

BEFORE LISTENING

PREDICTING   **A**   Look at the photo and read the caption. What do you think you will hear about this place? Discuss your prediction with a partner.

WHILE LISTENING

LISTENING FOR
MAIN IDEAS   **B**   🎧 1.38   Read the question and answer choices. Then listen to the conversation and choose the correct answer.

What did Maria think about her trip to the ICEHOTEL?

a. It was an amazing manmade place, but she didn't like the cold.
b. It was a place with a good mix of natural and manmade.
c. It was crowded with too many tourists.

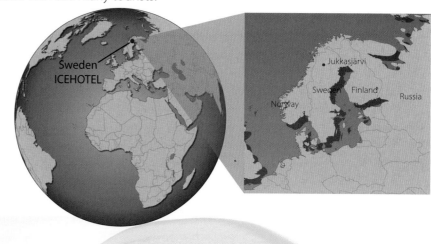

**Visitors in front of the Jukkasjärvi
ICEHOTEL in northern Sweden**

One way to listen and take notes is to listen for the answers to questions. This will help you understand the main ideas. When you listen to a story or a conversation, use a *wh-*question chart. Note the answers to questions like the ones in this chart.

Who?	Who are the important people?
What?	What happens?
Where?	Where does it happen?
When?	When does it happen?
Why?	Why does something happen?
How?	How does something happen?

C 🎧 1.38 Listen to the conversation again and take notes in the chart. Compare your charts in a small group and add information to your chart.

NOTE TAKING

Who?	Maria is talking to Juan about her vacation.
What?	
Where?	
When?	
Why?	
How?	

AFTER LISTENING

D Read the statements. Check (✓) the statements that you think are true. Then compare your answers with a partner. Explain your reasons for your answers.

CRITICAL THINKING: MAKING INFERENCES

1. _____ Maria goes to the ICEHOTEL every year.

2. _____ Maria likes to go to unknown places.

3. _____ The ICEHOTEL is open all year.

4. _____ You need warm clothes inside the ICEHOTEL.

5. _____ Maria's friends prefer normal vacations.

Speaking

PRONUNCIATION Syllables and Stress

🎧 1.39 Syllables are the smallest units of sound in a word. A syllable has at least one vowel sound and maybe one or more consonant sounds*. Listen to the examples.

One-syllable words	Two-syllable words	Three-syllable words
rice	*is-land*	*beau-ti-ful*
book	*ad-vice*	*a-ma-zing*

In words with two or more syllables, one syllable is stronger or *stressed*. This means the vowel sound is louder and clearer in the stressed syllable. Listen again to the words. Notice the stressed syllable.

One-syllable words	Two-syllable words	Three-syllable words
rice	**is**-land	**beau**-ti-ful
book	ad-**vice**	a-**ma**-zing

Pronouncing the correct stressed syllable is important for clear speech.

*Vowel sounds are made with the letters *a, e, i, o, u* and consonant sounds with all the other letters (*b, d, f, k, l, m,…*).

A 🎧 1.40 Listen and repeat the words. Write 1, 2, or 3 for the number of syllables.

1. hotel __2__
2. love __1__
3. vacation __3__
4. special __2__
5. area __2__

6. together __2__
7. view __1__
8. company __3__
9. manager __3__
10. famous __2__

B Check your answers to exercise A with a partner. Then take turns saying a word and telling which syllable is stressed. Underline the stressed syllable.

1. ho<u>tel</u>
2. love
3. vacation
4. special
5. area

6. together
7. view
8. company
9. manager
10. famous

Pair work and group work are common classroom activities. Use these expressions when working with other people.

Let's work together.   *Do you want to work together?*   *Can I ask you a question?*

Good idea!   *We need one more idea.*   *Can you help me?*

What do you think   *I'm not sure about that.*   *How about…?*
about…?

C Work in a small group. Discuss the question: *What are the pros and cons of taking a group tour?* Write your ideas in the chart. Use the Everyday Language phrases when discussing in your group.

CRITICAL THINKING: ANALYZING

Taking a Group Tour	
Pros	**Cons**

FINAL TASK Presenting Class Survey Results

You will take a survey of your classmates and find out what type of vacation they like or how they like to spend their time on vacation. You will create a bar graph with the results and then give a presentation to the rest of the class about the survey.

A Think of a question about vacation preferences to ask your classmates. Choose a pair of ideas from the box below to write your question or think of one on your own.

Example: (manmade/natural)
Do you like to go to a manmade destination or a natural destination on vacation?

alone/with friends	quiet/crowded	modern/old
exciting/educational	warm/cold	unusual/typical

Question: _____

B Walk around and ask your survey question to your classmates. Write notes in your notebook.

PRESENTATION SKILLS Presenting with Graphics

Using graphics in a presentation can help your audience understand the information more easily. Say these phrases when using graphics.

This graph shows . . .

As you can see from this graph, . . .

C Look at the sample presentation and bar graph.

> *Hello. I want to tell you about my survey. My question was: Do you like to go to manmade or natural destinations? I asked 15 people. As you can see from my graph, 11 people like to go to manmade destinations, and 4 people like to go to natural destinations.*

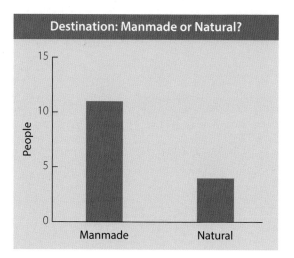

CRITICAL THINKING: INTERPRETING **D** Create a two-column bar graph showing the results of your survey on a separate piece of paper. Then practice your presentation.

PRESENTING **E** Give your presentation to the class. Remember to point to your graph.

REFLECTION

1. How can you use a pro and con chart to help you make decisions?

_____

_____

2. How do your own vacations compare with the places in the unit?

_____

_____

3. Here are the vocabulary words from the unit. Check (✓) the ones you can use.

☐ amazing	☐ manmade	☐ tourist
☐ area AWL	☐ mix	☐ unusual
☐ beautiful	☐ modern	☐ view
☐ crowded	☐ natural	☐ visit
☐ famous	☐ quiet	
☐ island	☐ special	

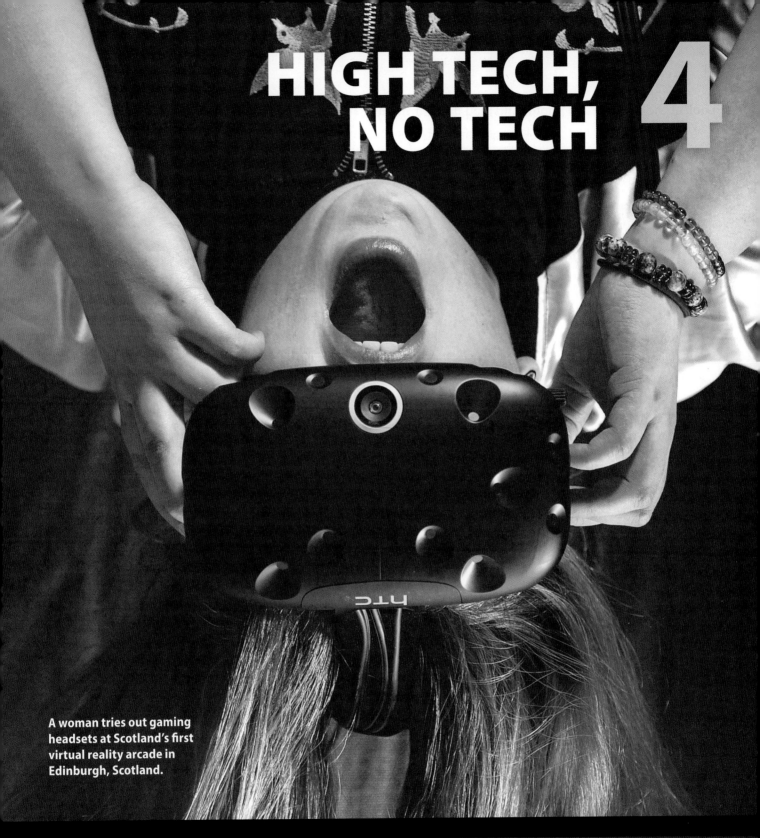

HIGH TECH, NO TECH 4

A woman tries out gaming headsets at Scotland's first virtual reality arcade in Edinburgh, Scotland.

THINK AND DISCUSS

1 What is the woman doing? Have you ever tried this?

2 How do you think she feels? What are some things she might be seeing (or experiencing)?

3 Why is virtual reality interesting to people? Do you think it's interesting? Explain.

Look at the timeline and photos and read the information. Then discuss the questions.

1. What does the timeline show? How are past telephones and cameras different from those today?

2. What are other tools or devices that were different in the past? Explain how they were different.

3. What do you think is the next step for phones, cameras, and other technologies?

HOW DID WE GET HERE?

One of the first phones and its inventor, Alexander Graham Bell

A telephone from the 1960s

1876

1960s

Over 1000 years ago

1948

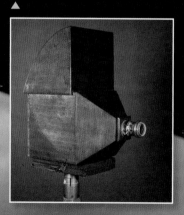

The Pinhole Camera was first invented long ago by Ibn Al-Haytham, who was born in Iraq in 965AD.

The first instant camera

Vestrahorn Stokksnes,
Iceland

Mano tech → very small tech

ting → the same At&t

The first mobile phone
weighed 2.4lbs (1.1kg). With this
model, you got 30 minutes
of talk-time. It took about 10 hours
to charge.

1973

1983

An early video camera
recorder (camcorder)

A Vocabulary

A 🎧 **1.41** Listen and check the words you already know. Then discuss their meaning with a partner. Check the dictionary for any you are not sure about.

☐ benefit *(n)*   ☐ equipment *(n)*   ☐ hard *(adj)*   ☐ prepare *(v)*

☐ download *(v)*   ☐ experience *(v)*   ☐ the past *(n)*   ☐ real *(adj)*

MEANING FROM CONTEXT

B 🎧 **1.42** Listen to the podcast. Complete the information with the words you hear from exercise A.

AMERICA'S NATIONAL PARKS GO VIRTUAL

Today, you can go on a journey through the national parks and __experience__ (1) the beauty without ever leaving your home. Some national parks in the United States have a virtual reality (VR) tour. You do not need to __prepare__ (2) for a long trip any more. It's not __hard__ (3) at all; it's very easy. You can just __download__ (4) the National Park VR app, put on some VR glasses, and in no time, you feel like you are in Yosemite National Park. It is always better to see the __real__ (5) thing, but a VR tour allows anyone to see the park at any time! It can cost a lot of money to visit the parks, so the VR tour gives you the opportunity to experience the beautiful views without spending a lot. In __the past__ (6), the only ways to see the parks were to travel there, look at photos, or watch a video. Another __benefit__ (7) of visiting the park virtually is that it will not be crowded. Any time you are ready, just put on your VR __equipment__ (8) and go!

The moon rises over Half Dome in Yosemite National Park, California.

C Write the correct word from exercise A next to its definition.

1. ~~Explor~~ *benefit* — a good thing
2. *Download* — to put something on your computer or phone
3. *prepare* — to plan
4. *Experience* — to do or feel
5. *real* — genuine, not false ⟸ *authentic*
6. *equipment* — tools or devices
7. *hard* — difficult ⟸ *not easy.*
8. *the past* — the time before now

VOCABULARY SKILL Adjective Order

Adjectives are words that describe something or someone. When you want to use more than one adjective in a sentence, they come in a certain order. For example, an adjective that describes an opinion about something comes before an adjective that describes the age of something.

> I just bought an **amazing new** phone.
> Have you played this **exciting new** game?
> I'm tired of this **boring old** flip phone.

D Write the words in the correct order for each sentence.

1. Virtual reality is better than ~~video~~ *boring old videos.* (boring / videos / old).
2. Please download this ~~app~~ *cool new app* (new / app / cool).
3. With virtual reality, you can see *beautiful old things* (old / beautiful / things) from the past.
4. This company uses some *amazing modern equipment* (equipment / modern / amazing).

E Discuss the questions in a small group.

1. What are the benefits of seeing something in virtual reality? What are the benefits of seeing the real thing?
   - outside. because interactive with another children
2. Name something that was better in the past. Why was it better?
   - children complay ~~with another child~~
3. What are some benefits of technology? How does it make your life easy?
   - Talk with my mother with video every day GPS
4. What equipment do you need for school? For home?
   - Laptop / computer / cameras / phones.
   - TV
   - computer
   - Robot vaccum for clean the house.
   - laundry machine. and dryer

Handwritten margin notes:
- Overachiever → to be achiever more than need necessary.
- Redundant → every day the same thing
- Narrow → thin
- 1) Determiner a, an, both, some, many
- 2) Opinion good, great, beautiful
- 3) Size huge, big, tiny large, little
- 4) Shape rectangular
- 5) Age/time new, modern
- 6) Color blue, red, pink
- Benefit
- VR: more cheaper, more continent, less crowded
- Real thing: Know the different places, meet people, face to face

Listening A Conversation about Virtual Reality

BEFORE LISTENING

PREVIEWING **A** What is the student in the photo doing? What equipment do you need for this activity? What do you know about the activity? Discuss your ideas with a partner.

A teen tests a virtual reality headset in Copenhagen, Denmark.

A virtual reality headset with mobile phone and headphones

WHILE LISTENING

LISTENING FOR MAIN IDEAS **B** 🎧 1.43 Listen to two friends talk about virtual reality. Choose the correct answer to complete the main idea.

1. The conversation between Paul and Lily is mainly about _____.
   a. how virtual reality works in real life
   b. how virtual reality can be used in a classroom
   c. how to prepare for a presentation
   d. how a company creates the lessons for the classroom

2. Virtual reality is _____.
   a. great for the classroom
   b. just for gaming
   c. for young students only
   d. bad for people's eyes

3. Virtual reality is a benefit to schools because _____.
   a. it can take anyone anywhere at any time
   b. it is easy to use
   c. students can experience things without leaving the classroom
   d. all of the above

4. What process does Paul tell Lily about?
   a. how to prepare for a presentation
   b. how to give students a real experience in class
   c. how to make your own virtual reality headset
   d. how to use virtual reality

LISTENING SKILL Listening for Steps in a Process

Speakers use certain words before they list the steps in a process. If you hear one of these words, be sure to take notes.

First, …	*Second, …*	*Third, …*	*Last, …*
Next, …	*Then, …*	*After that, …*	*Finally, …*

C 🎧 1.44 Listen to the excerpt from the conversation and complete the steps with the correct words or phrases.

First, _____ an app on your phone.
⟨1⟩

Second, put your _____ in the headset.
⟨2⟩

Third, put the headset on so it _____ well on your _____.
⟨3⟩ ⟨4⟩

Finally, use your controller to _____ the _____ and begin.
⟨5⟩ ⟨6⟩

D 🎧 1.43 Listen to the complete conversation again. Choose the correct answers.

LISTENING FOR DETAILS

1. Paul is preparing to _____.
   a. give a presentation
   b. take a virtual reality class
   c. create a virtual reality lesson

2. Which example of virtual reality does Paul NOT mention?
   a. Students can see the Himalayan Mountains.
   b. Students can touch the Eiffel Tower.
   c. Students can swim with blue whales.

3. What are the four things you need to experience virtual reality?
   a. a computer, a phone, a headset, an app
   b. a TV, a controller, a phone, a DVD
   c. a phone, a controller, a headset, an app

4. What does Paul say you can make a headset out of?
   a. plastic
   b. cardboard
   c. wood

AFTER LISTENING

E Work in a small group. Think of activities that you can do with virtual reality for these school subjects: *language learning, history, math, science*. Then discuss which subject will have the biggest benefit from virtual reality. Share an idea with the class.

CRITICAL THINKING: APPLYING

> *You can use virtual reality to experience important events in history. For example, maybe you can experience walking on the moon.*

HIGH TECH, NO TECH **67**

A Speaking

GRAMMAR FOR SPEAKING *Can* and *Can't*

Can is a modal verb. A modal comes before the base form of a verb. Modals add information to a verb. Use *can* to talk about ability or possibility.

> Students **can experience** history with virtual reality, but they **can't touch** anything.

The negative form of *can* is *cannot* or *can't*. *Can't* is usually used in spoken English.

> Schools **cannot pay** to send all their students to Paris this year.
> Students **can't travel** abroad every year, but they can travel to nearby places.

PRONUNCIATION *Can* and *Can't*

🎧 1.45 In a sentence, the word *can* is usually unstressed. That means the vowel is reduced to schwa /kən/ or omitted completely /kn/. The word *can't* is usually stressed and has the full vowel sound /kænt/.

> Kuri can **talk** to people and move around the house.
> Kuri **can't** pick things up or clean your house.

▶ **Kuri, a robot that smiles and is "friendly," talks with a young girl.**

A Work with a partner. Partner A, look at the chart below. Partner B, look at the chart on the next page. Take turns telling your partner what the robot can (O) and can't (X) do. Listen and write your partner's information.

Partner A: The home robot/Kuri…		Partner B: The home robot/Kuri…	
O	move around your home		
X	wash floors		
O	read a book to you		
X	bring things to you		
O	take pictures and video		

Partner A: The home robot/Kuri…		Partner B: The home robot/Kuri…	
		O	play music
		X	clean your house
		O	know who is in your family
		X	speak English
		O	greet you when you come home

B Find three kinds of robots on the Internet. Complete the chart with each robot and the things they can and can't do. Share your most interesting robot with a partner.

Type of Robot	Can	Can't
vacuum cleaner (like Roomba®)	clean floors	go over big electrical wires

C With your class, discuss the things you can and can't do with a book and an e-book. Write one more example for each. Share your ideas with your class.

CRITICAL THINKING: ANALYZING

Equipment	Can	Can't
Books	*touch the book*	*carry many books easily*
	_____	_____
E-books	*have many books at one time*	*read without electricity*
	_____	_____

A man sits in a hammock and reads a book outside the closed door of a shop in Vietnam.

SPEAKING SKILL Giving Reasons

To give reasons for something, we often use words such as *because* and *since*. These words can come at the beginning or in the middle of a sentence. If we use the word at the beginning of a sentence, we put a comma after the reason. In speaking, a comma is often a short pause.

*Virtual reality is good for the classroom **because** it is not expensive.*
***Since** I have a hard time going to sleep, I listen to music at night.*

D Do you live a modern life? Read and discuss the situations below with a small group. Discuss the reasons for your answers.

1. You work at a store. Your boss tells you that you can stay at home and use a robot to do your work. Do you decide to work from home or do you go to the store as usual? Give reasons for your answer.

2. Your school offers the same classes online that you take at school. Do you take the online course or do you continue to go to school? Explain.

3. Your school has a trip to the Grand Canyon. It is very expensive. You can also stay in school and take the virtual reality tour. Which do you choose? Why?

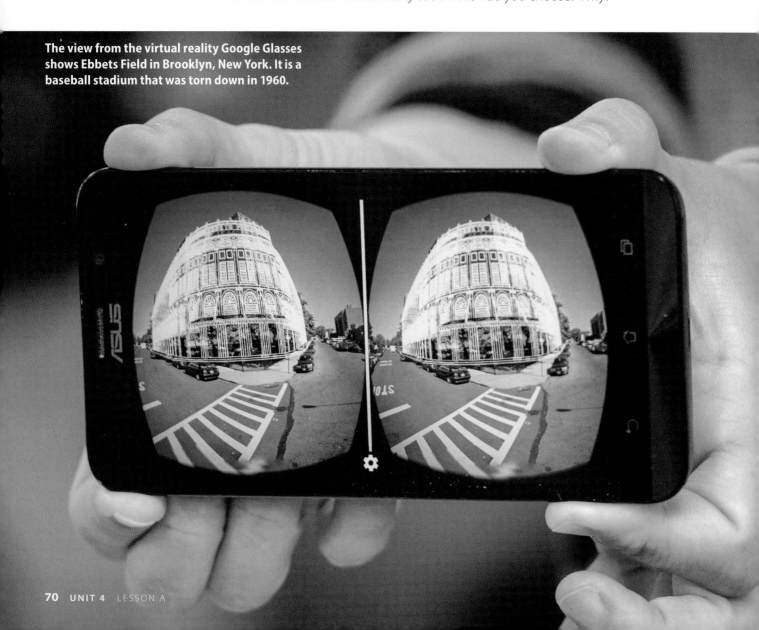

The view from the virtual reality Google Glasses shows Ebbets Field in Brooklyn, New York. It is a baseball stadium that was torn down in 1960.

LESSON TASK Presenting a New Tech Device

A Work with a partner to create a new technology. Discuss the categories in the chart and start to plan your technology.

Tell the type of technology (machine, digital, computer, robot)	
Explain what your technology is for (education, entertainment, health, business, home life, school life)	
Describe what your technology can do	
Give your technology a name	

B Share your idea with the class. Use the following as a model for sharing your idea.

Our new technology is _____.

It is for _____.

This technology can _____.

We named it _____.

Our technology is necessary because _____.

C Vote for the best technology. Write the names of the technology you vote for in each category. Then take a class vote to determine the best overall.

1. Most creative _____

2. Most useful _____

3. Most interesting/fun _____

4. I want one right now! _____

Video

A man takes a selfie from the top of a mountain in Washington State, USA.

High Tech or No Tech?

▶ **US National Parks**

BEFORE VIEWING

A Match each word or phrase from the video with its definition. Use your dictionary to help you.

1. _____ generation
2. _____ be wrapped up
3. _____ occupy time
4. _____ accessible
5. _____ authentic
6. _____ unplug
7. _____ enemy

a. to do something so you are not bored
b. easy to find or experience
c. stop using technology
d. be thinking about something all the time
e. people born around the same time
f. a person or a thing that can hurt you
g. real

B Check (✓) the social media, Internet sites, and technology that you use. Share your answer with a partner. How do you compare?

☐ WhatsApp   ☐ Facebook   ☐ GPS   ☐ Twitter   ☐ YouTube

☐ drones   ☐ Google Maps   ☐ Instagram   ☐ virtual reality   ☐ _____

C Look at the photo. What is the man doing? With your partner, brainstorm other things you can do with technology in parks. Write ideas in your notebook.

WHILE VIEWING

D ▶ 1.7 Watch the video. Choose the correct answer for each.

UNDERSTANDING MAIN IDEAS

1. The video is about how _____.
   a. technology is not allowed in national parks
   b. the use of technology can be good and bad in national parks
   c. it is important to prepare your technology before visiting the national parks

2. The people in the video _____.
   a. give examples of how to use technology in the park
   b. complain that there is no Wi-Fi in the parks
   c. want to use equipment from the past

E ▶ 1.7 Watch the video again. Check (✓) the ways in which people in the video say they use technology in national parks.

UNDERSTANDING DETAILS

_____ Instagram   _____ look at trails   _____ research

_____ Tweet   _____ look at birding apps   _____ play games

_____ take pictures   _____ use Google Maps to find parks

AFTER VIEWING

F Read the comments based on comments from the video. Decide which are *Pro* and which are *Against* technology in national parks. Write P for *Pro* or A for *Against*.

CRITICAL THINKING: EVALUATING

_____ 1. Technology can help bring people into parks if you let them know…

_____ 2. People are afraid to be alone in nature without anything to occupy their time.

_____ 3. I love that social media can capture those moments.

_____ 4. People see images of these places. It makes them want to go.

_____ 5. There's a lot of visitors that come here that are so wrapped up in technology…

_____ 6. That's when they start to realize there's more to life than technology.

G Work in a small group. Compare your responses to exercise F. Explain your reasons for any different answers. Remember to use *because* or *since* when giving a reason.

B Vocabulary

A 🎧 1.46 Listen and check (✓) the words you already know.

☐ available *(adj)*   ☐ depend on *(v)*   ☐ health *(n)*   ☐ rest *(n)*
☐ brain *(n)*   ☐ effect *(n)*   ☐ hurt *(v)*   ☐ worry *(v)*

MEANING FROM
CONTEXT

B 🎧 1.47 Read and listen to *Technology News Now*. Complete the story with the words you hear.

TECHNOLOGY NEWS NOW

Beware! Your cell phone can be bad for your _____! Nowadays, we
_____ our cell phones for everything. We use them to check email, send
texts, do work, watch movies, listen to music, play games, and even pay our bills.
We are always online. We are _____ for our bosses, our friends, and our
families 24 hours a day, 7 days a week. Doctors now say that all of this technology can
_____ us.

If you want to do something about this, give your _____ a break! Go
outside. Go to the park. Take a walk. The fresh air, the beautiful sky, and the trees help
give you the _____ you need. So, for your next lunch break, go and enjoy
the _____ of the sunshine. And leave your cell phone at your desk. Don't
_____ — the world can wait!

C Write the correct word from exercise A to complete each sentence.

1. I _____ my hand last week, and now I can't use my computer.

2. Be sure to take a break from technology every day. It can have a bad _____ on you.

3. Some say technology can hurt a teenager's _____ because it is still growing.

4. Some people _____ that virtual reality is bad for people's eyes.

5. I eat lunch outside every day. The sky and trees give me the _____ I need!

6. I have to be _____ for my job seven days a week, either by phone or email.

7. People _____ their cell phones for everything. They can't live without them!

8. Some helpful advice for good _____ is to go outside more.

Two women pose for a selfie in Manila, the Philippines.

CRITICAL THINKING   Interpreting a Bar Graph

Follow these steps to understand the information on a bar graph:

1. Read the title of the graph (*Minutes per Day on Devices*).
2. Read the labels under the bars (*TV, Laptop,...*) and the scale (numbers on the side).
3. Compare the height of the bars to understand the information. (People spend more time watching TV or using their smartphones.)

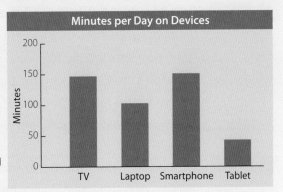

D   Work with a partner. Look at the bar graph and answer the questions.

CRITICAL THINKING: INTERPRETING

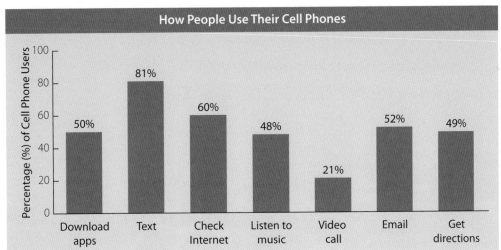

1. What percentage of people check the Internet on their phone? _____
2. What activity do 81 percent of people do with their phone? _____
3. What activity do people do the least with their phone? _____
4. What percentage of people listen to music on their phone? _____
5. What are the top three things people use their phone for? _____
   _____ , _____

E   Look again at the bar graph in exercise D. Do you use your cell phone in the same way? Create your own bar graph about your phone usage. Discuss your graphs in a small group.

CRITICAL THINKING: APPLYING

Listening Class Discussion: Taking a Tech Break

A Think about the bad effects technology can have on our health. List your ideas and then discuss them with a partner.

_____

_____

WHILE LISTENING

LISTENING FOR
MAIN IDEAS

B 🎧 1.48 Listen to a class discussion and check (✓) the two main ideas you hear.

1. _____ Different generations use different types of technology.
2. _____ Using your smartphone too much can have bad effects.
3. _____ It is good to take a break from our phones.
4. _____ Being available for people on your phone is difficult.
5. _____ Life was better in the past when we didn't have smartphones.

LISTENING FOR
DETAILS

C 🎧 1.48 Listen again. Write T for *True* or F for *False*.

1. Some people are on their phones five hours a day. _____
2. The teacher is going to discuss four bad effects of using a smartphone. _____
3. The light on a screen makes people tired. _____
4. 24/7/365 is the amount of time people are on their phones. _____
5. It's important for your brain to remember things. _____
6. Stress is one bad effect that phones have on the body. _____

A man rests and enjoys a view of the Rocky Mountains in Yellowstone National Park, Montana, USA.

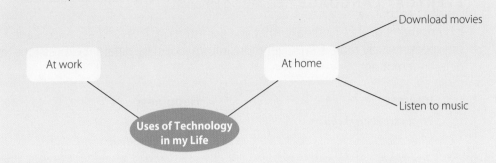
D 🎧 1.49 Listen to an excerpt from the class discussion and complete the spider map. Use the ideas in the box and your own ideas.

NOTE TAKING

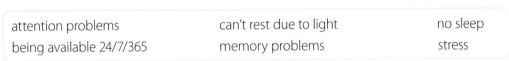

| attention problems | can't rest due to light | no sleep |
| being available 24/7/365 | memory problems | stress |

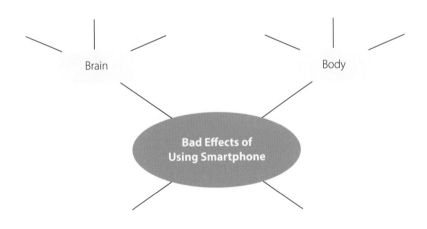

AFTER LISTENING

E Work in a small group. Discuss the following questions.

PERSONALIZING

1. Do you like to be available 24 hours a day, 7 days a week, 365 days a year? Do you like your friends, classmates, or co-workers to be available? Explain your answer.

2. When do you unplug, or turn off technology? For how long? Why?

3. Do you depend on technology? How?

F With a partner, add information to the spider map in exercise D. Then share your ideas with another pair.

CRITICAL THINKING: SYNTHESIZING

Speaking

EVERYDAY LANGUAGE Expressing Emotion

It is important to show a speaker that you are listening. This can help encourage the speaker to say more so you get more information. Use different expressions for different emotions.

Interest	**Happiness**
That's so interesting!	*Wonderful!*
How cool!	*I'm happy to hear that!*
Amazing!	
Surprise	**Sadness**
Really?	*That's so terrible.*
Are you serious?	*I'm sorry to hear that.*

A 🎧 1.50 Listen and complete the conversation with the Everyday Language phrases you hear. Then compare your answers with a partner. Together, decide which emotion the listener is trying to express.

A: Are you using any new apps on your phone?

B: Yes, I really like my new walking app. I use it at the gym.

A: (1) _____ Tell me about it.   (Emotion: _____)

B: It's called Virtual Walk™. First, you download the app on your phone. Then you choose a place where you want to walk. You can choose a national park to walk through. You can walk to all of the monuments in Washington, D.C. There are lots of places to choose.

A: (2) _____   (Emotion: _____)

B: Next, you get on your treadmill, put on your virtual reality headset, and turn on your app. Then you walk. The virtual reality makes you feel like you are walking in the real place.

A: (3) _____ It feels real?   (Emotion: _____)

B: Yes. It's a lot of fun. But you have to be careful. You can't see the real world with your virtual reality headset on, so sometimes you can fall down.

A: (4) _____ Did that happen to you?   (Emotion: _____)

B: Yes, and I hurt my arm.

A: (5) _____   (Emotion: _____)

B Think of an app that you use. Tell your partner about it. When you listen to your partner, show interest by using one of the Everyday Language expressions.

C Think of the following areas of your life: *Home, Work, School, Health, Entertainment, Hobby*. On spider map A, take notes on the technology that you use for each area of your life. Take turns explaining your use of technology to a partner. Take notes on your partner's information on spider map B.

Spider Map A

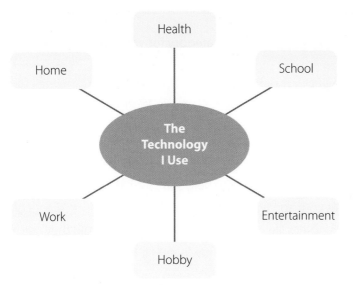

Spider Map B

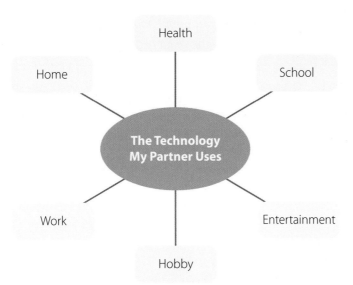

D With your partner, discuss the questions about your spider map notes from exercise C.   PERSONALIZING

1. Is there an area of your life where you use too much technology? Not enough?

2. What devices do you use in most areas of your life (e.g., cell phone, tablet)?

3. In which areas of your life are you and your partner very similar? Very different?

4. Do you want to change how you use technology in your life?

FINAL TASK Presenting a New App

> With a partner, you will create an idea for an app. Then you will present your app to the class as a part of a "New Technology Fair." Try to find pictures or create a picture of the app's features. If possible, give a demonstration of the app for your presentation.

A Work with a partner. Choose a category for your app or write in your own choice.

Entertainment	Hobby	School	Your choice
Health	Home	Work	_____

BRAINSTORMING **B** Think of an idea for an app for the category from exercise A. Create a spider map or a *wh*-question chart in your notebook to help you note answers to these questions.

1. What problem does your app help solve? What does it do?
2. Who uses your app (your "target user")?
3. Why is the user's life easier with your app? Why should they use it?
4. How do you use the app? Or how easy is it to use?

PRESENTATION SKILL Getting People's Attention

At a job or technology fair, there are many people walking around. In order to get them to come to your table, you need to get their attention. It is good to be specific about the information you want to share.

Hi! Check out this cool restaurant app!
Hello! Let me show you this great health app!

PRESENTING **C** Present your ideas at a class "New Technology Fair." One partner presents your app to students at the "fair." The other walks around and listens to other presentations. After five minutes, switch roles. Remember to get people's attention. Use the phrases for giving reasons to tell people why it is good. As you listen to other presentations, use the Everyday Language expressions to show interest.

REFLECTION

1. How can spider maps help you keep your notes organized?

_____

_____

2. Overall, do you think technology is good or bad for you? Explain.

_____

_____

3. Here are the vocabulary words from the unit. Check (✓) the ones you can use.

☐ available AWL	☐ equipment AWL	☐ real
☐ benefit AWL	☐ experience	☐ rest
☐ brain	☐ hard	☐ the past
☐ depend on	☐ health	☐ worry
☐ download	☐ hurt	
☐ effect	☐ prepare	

RISK AND REWARD 5

Surfer among sharks,
KwaZulu-Natal, South Africa

THINK AND DISCUSS

1 What is the person in the photo doing? Where is this?
2 Why is the person doing it?
3 Do you want to try this activity? Why or why not?

Look at the photos and read the information. Then discuss the questions.

1. What is each person doing? What are the risks?
2. What are other ways people take risks at work or for fun?
3. Why do people take risks? What are possible rewards?

EXTREME RISK

People often **take risks**. Some people do an extreme sport, such as bungee jumping, for fun. Others take risks just by doing their jobs every day.

Just another day at work for National Geographic Explorer, climber, and photographer Jimmy Chin, Yosemite National Park

An expert holds a deadly sea snake in Fijian waters. Though these snakes don't usually attack humans, their bite can kill.

A woman bungee jumps backwards at The Last Resort in Nepal.

A Vocabulary

A 🎧 2.2 Listen and check (✓) the words you already know. Then discuss their meaning with a partner. Check the dictionary for any you are not sure about.

☐ adventure (*n*)	☐ climb (*v*)	☐ difficult (*adj*)	☐ solve (*v*)
☐ body (*n*)	☐ die (*v*)	☐ mind (*n*)	☐ vote (*v*)

MEANING FROM
CONTEXT

B 🎧 2.3 Look at the photo and read the caption. Complete the conversations with the words in exercise A. Then listen and correct your answers.

Conversation 1

A: I'm planning to _____ K2 next year.
    ₁

B: Wow! That sounds like a real _____ .
    ₂

A: Yes, but it's going to be _____ . I have to train every day to get ready.
    ₃

B: Well, be careful. You can _____ in the mountains if you're not in shape.
    ₄

Conversation 2

A: It's important to do different exercises so your whole _____ becomes
    ₅
stronger, not just your arms, but also your legs, back, and so on.

B: Many people say you should exercise to help your _____ , too.
    ₆

A: Yes. Absolutely. Exercise helps me think a lot more clearly.

Conversation 3

A: Did you _____ for the new class president?
    ₇

B: Yes, I did. Let's hope the winner can _____ some of the problems
    ₈
we're having at school.

C Write the correct word from exercise A next to its definition.

1. _____ the form (head, arms, legs,…) of a person or animal

2. _____ not easy

3. _____ a person's thoughts, feelings, ideas

4. _____ to find the answer to a question or problem

5. _____ to move up

6. _____ an exciting time or event

7. _____ to choose a person or thing to win some position or prize

8. _____ to stop living

Climbers on the Chinese side of K2, the second highest mountain in the world after Mount Everest

VOCABULARY SKILL Noun Suffixes -er and -ing

A suffix is one or more letters that come at the end of certain words. They indicate the meaning and part of speech of the word. Common suffixes that form nouns are -er (usually a person or doer of an activity) and -ing (an activity).

Note: An -ing noun form is also called a gerund.

> climb (verb): climb**er** (noun, person who does the sport)
>
> climb**ing** (noun, the sport)

D Choose the correct answer to complete the sentences.

1. The (explorer / exploring) loves the ocean. He is both a (diver / diving) and a (photographer / photographing).
2. My favorite sports are (runner / running) and (swimmer / swimming).
3. I want to be a famous piano (player / playing) one day.
4. (Surfer / Surfing) is a difficult sport to learn, but my sister is a great (teacher / teaching).

E Discuss the questions with a small group.   PERSONALIZING

1. Give an example of an adventure you are interested in.
2. Imagine you are one of the climbers in the photo. How do you feel? What are some risks of doing this climb? What are the possible rewards?
3. Do you want to climb K2 or Mt. Everest one day? Explain why or why not.

Listening
Podcast: Adventurer of the Year

**Pasang Lhamu Sherpa Akita
climbing a rock route,
Hattiban, Nepal**

BEFORE LISTENING

PREVIEWING **A** Look at the photo and read the information.
Discuss the questions with a partner.

1. Where is Pasang Lhamu Sherpa Akita from?
2. What does she do?
3. How do you think someone becomes
   Adventurer of the Year?

▲ **Pasang Lhamu Sherpa Akita is
a climber and mountain guide
from Nepal. She was National
Geographic's People's Choice
Adventurer of the Year, 2016.**

WHILE LISTENING

LISTENING FOR
MAIN IDEAS
B 🎧 2.4 ▶ 1.8 Listen to the podcast and choose the correct answer to complete each
main idea.

1. According to Gina, an adventurer _____ .

   a. is not afraid of anything

   b. loves extreme sports

   c. can be different things

2. Adventurer of the Year is a yearly
   award _____ .

   a. for sports

   b. from National Geographic

   c. for mountain climbers

3. Pasang Lhamu Sherpa Akita _____ .

   a. is a mountain guide and one of the
      first Nepali females to climb K2

   b. is a role model for girls in Nepal

   c. helped people during the 2015
      earthquake

   d. all of the above

A speaker uses certain words or phrases before giving examples. If you hear one of these words or phrases, be sure to take notes. The information after them usually supports the speaker's idea.

> *For example, …*
> *…such as…*
> *…like…*

C 🎧 **2.5** Listen to the excerpts from the interview and complete the sentences with the correct words or phrases.

1. An adventurer is often someone who does a dangerous or *extreme* sport
   _____ mountain climbing, _____ , or highlining.

2. But someone can be adventurous in their work, too. _____
   photographers take pictures of interesting people and places, and
   _____ travel all over the world and discover many things.

3. Sure! The Adventurer of the Year in 2016, _____ , was Pasang Lhamu
   Sherpa Akita. She's a mountain _____ from Nepal. She was one of the
   first Nepali women to _____ K2.…

D 🎧 **2.4** Listen again to the complete interview. Choose the correct answers.

LISTENING FOR DETAILS

1. Gina Inaka is a _____ .
   a. reporter
   b. adventurer
   c. podcaster

2. National Geographic chooses _____ adventurers each year.
   a. 5
   b. 10
   c. 15

3. _____ vote for the Adventurer of the Year each year.
   a. National Geographic workers
   b. People anywhere
   c. Students

4. In 2015, a terrible _____ hit Nepal.
   a. earthquake
   b. storm
   c. wind

5. Over _____ people died.
   a. 800
   b. 8,000
   c. 8 million

6. You can go to the National Geographic website now and vote for _____ .
   a. 10 adventurers
   b. Gina's podcast
   c. one adventurer

AFTER LISTENING

E Work in a small group. Look at the activities. What are possible risks and rewards of each? Choose one and explain your ideas to the group.

CRITICAL THINKING: REFLECTING

| exercising | going to college | teaching | traveling |

A Speaking

A 🎧 2.6 Listen to the excerpts from the podcast on page 86. Write the missing expressions. Then practice the conversations with a partner.

1. Michael: So, first, can you tell everyone what the Adventurer of the Year award is?

   Gina: _____ ! Each year, National Geographic chooses 10 of the best…

2. Gina: But they also need to solve problems and think quickly, so a good mind is important, too.

   Michael: _____ ! Great points. So, who votes?

3. Michael: I see. Can you give us an example? Tell us about one of the winners.

   Gina: _____ ! The Adventurer of the Year in 2016, for example, was Pasang…

4. Michael: And she takes risks to help others. A true adventurer.

   Gina: _____ !

CRITICAL THINKING:
INTERPRETING A CHART

B With your partner, look at the chart and take turns asking and answering questions about what each person likes. Use different words for *yes* and *no*.

A: *Does Mike like climbing mountains?*
B: *Are you kidding? No way.*

Activity	Mike	Jana	Tamas
1. climbing mountains	no	no	yes
2. singing karaoke with friends	no	no	yes
3. writing a poem in English	yes	yes	no
4. running a long-distance race	no	no	yes
5. speaking in front of a large audience	no	yes	yes

C Discuss the questions with your partner.

1. Which person in the chart above takes the most risks? The least?
2. Who are you most similar to?

D Work with a new partner. Ask your partner the questions on the quiz and mark your partner's answers. Use different words for *Yes* and *No*.

QUIZ: ARE YOU A RISK-TAKER?

	Yes	No
1. Your friend asks you to try skydiving. Do you try it?	☐	☐
2. Your friend asks you to take a rock-climbing lesson. Do you try it?	☐	☐
3. Your friend asks you to try food from a foreign country. It's a new food for you. Do you try it?	☐	☐
4. You are offered a great job, but you don't have the skills for it. Do you take the job?	☐	☐
5. Someone gives you a free trip to the International Space Station. Do you go?	☐	☐
6. Someone asks you to sing a song at a school event. Do you do it?	☐	☐

Count how many times you marked *yes* for your partner. _____

E Is your partner a risk-taker? Use the Key to find your partner's score. Take turns telling your partner his/her score and reading the description. Do you agree with your results?

Key: **5–6:** You are very adventurous and a risk-taker! You love to try new things and aren't afraid to fail.

3–4: You are brave, but careful. You will try some new things, but not all.

0–2: You are not really a risk-taker. You like to be safe and stay close to home.

Skydiving instructor with a student

SPEAKING SKILL Giving Examples

Examples help support your ideas. To give examples when you speak, use these phrases: *for example*, *like*, and *such as*.

> I'm adventurous. **For example,** I love to climb trees.
> I enjoy activities **like** tennis, reading, and relaxing on the beach.
> I want to visit unusual places **such as** Antarctica and jungles in Africa.

GIVING EXAMPLES **F** Work with a new partner. Tell him or her the results of your quiz from page 89. Do you agree with the results? Give examples to support your opinion.

> **>** *I am brave, but careful. This is true. For example, I try different foods, and I'm not afraid to try a new job and learn it, but I won't bungee jump EVER.*

PERSONALIZING **G** Do you take risks with food? Look at the four foods from around the world. Discuss the questions with your partner.

1. Which of these foods do you know about? Have you ever eaten any of them?

2. Do you want to try any of them? Which ones?

3. What is the most unusual food you have tried?

4. What is a risk of trying unusual food? What is a possible reward?

▶ **(left) Durian is popular in Southeast Asia. The smell is so strong that many hotels do not allow it.**

▶ **(right) A street vendor displays fried insects in Bangkok, Thailand.**

▶ **(left) Black pudding, made of blood, is popular for breakfast in the U.K. and Ireland.**

▶ **(right) Kangaroo meat is a special food from Australia.**

LESSON TASK Presenting a Personal Plan

A Work with a small group. Look at the categories. For each one, discuss different ways to become more adventurous. Take notes in the chart. Remember to use different words for *yes* and *no* when you discuss ideas.

BRAINSTORMING

A: *We can try a different international food each month.*
B: *Definitely! And we can have a dinner party and each cook a new dish.*

Category	Ideas for Being More Adventurous
Food	*try international foods; cook new dish*
School/Career	
Travel	
Sports/Exercise	
Your Idea:	

B Choose one category where you want to become more adventurous. Complete the plan. List some of the things you will do and how often you will do them.

ORGANIZING IDEAS

My Plan to Become More Adventurous

Introduction: The area where I want to be more adventurous is _____ .

Steps: These are some of the different ways I'm going to become more adventurous.

> I will _____ every day/week/month.

> Also, I will _____

and _____ .

Conclusion: With this plan, I'm going to become more adventurous by _____ .
(date)

C Share your plan with your group. Use expressions from page 90 to introduce examples.

PRESENTING

> *I want to be more adventurous with travel. For example, I want to go to China.*

Video

Dean Potter
highlining in Yosemite
with a full moon

Highlining
Yosemite Falls

0   50
MILES

Yosemite National Park

● San Francisco

Yosemite Valley and
Glacier Point ●

**California
(U.S.)**

Pacific Ocean

BEFORE VIEWING

A Look at the photo and the map. Then discuss
these questions with a partner.

1. What is Dean Potter doing in the photo?

2. What is Yosemite? Where is it?

3. Do you want to try this? Explain.

B Match each word from the video with its definition. Use your dictionary to help you.

1. _____ line (n)
2. _____ (water) falls (n)
3. _____ wind (n)
4. _____ failure (n)
5. _____ focus (v)
6. _____ beauty (n)
7. _____ challenge (n)

a. natural moving air outside
b. an activity or plan that does not succeed
c. a long rope or cable that people walk across
d. to think only about the thing you are doing
e. water in mountains that goes down over rocks
f. a hard thing to do or a problem you have
g. something you look at that pleases you

WHILE VIEWING

C ▶ 1.9 Watch the video. Mark each statement **T** for *True* or **F** for *False*.

1. At the time of the video, Dean Potter lived in Yosemite Valley. **T F**
2. The line he walks on is strong. **T F**
3. Dean Potter doesn't have any trouble walking this line. **T F**
4. The weather and the waterfall are a difficult challenge for Dean. **T F**
5. Dean highlines because he loves to feel afraid. **T F**

D ▶ 1.9 Check your answers to exercise C with a partner. Discuss a correct statement for each *False* one. Watch the video again if necessary.

AFTER VIEWING

> **CRITICAL THINKING** Paraphrasing
>
> When you paraphrase, you say someone else's words in a different way. Paraphrasing is important:
> - to help you understand someone's words better.
> - to use during a presentation or other talk so you do not steal or copy (*plagiarize*) someone else's words, thoughts, or ideas.

E Work in a small group. Read Dean Potter's words. Discuss the meaning and agree on a paraphrase of it for the class.

... brief moments when you're just seeing everything, seeing the beautiful world, all that's there, right in the moment.

F Dean Potter says this about highlining: "… pushing into the unknown is a big part of what I call fun. Seeing a new part of yourself that you didn't know was there." In what way do you "push into the unknown"?

PERSONALIZING

B Vocabulary

A 🎧 **2.7** Listen and check (✓) the words you already know.

☐ count (v)   ☐ decrease (v)   ☐ forest (n)   ☐ protect (v)

☐ danger (n)   ☐ discover (v)   ☐ goals (n)   ☐ wild (adj)

MEANING FROM
CONTEXT

B 🎧 **2.8** Read and listen to the article. Notice each word in blue and think about its meaning.

> **EXPLORATION: RISK AND REWARD**
>
> Hundreds of years ago, people built boats and crossed the oceans. In the 1960s, astronauts started traveling to space. And today, people continue to go to new places and do things no one has done before. These people risk their lives. Why? What are their **goals**? Here are a few:
>
> - To learn: An explorer might face **danger** deep under the ocean, in a thick tropical rain **forest**, high on a mountain, or even in space in order to learn. Humans naturally want to learn.
>
> - To teach: When explorers **discover** something and learn about it, they teach us interesting new things. We learn not only about the world, but also about ourselves.
>
> - To **protect**: When a photographer takes a photo of a crocodile or some other **wild** animal, the animal becomes more real to us. We want to keep it safe. We **count** how many there are because we don't want the population to **decrease**.
>
> Everyone has goals. For many people, learning a job, teaching their children, and protecting their families and homes is enough. But for explorers, it's about changing the world.

C Write the correct word from exercise A next to its definition.

1. _____ things you want to do

2. _____ to see how many

3. _____ to become smaller in size

4. _____ a situation where something bad can happen to you

5. _____ to keep something or someone safe

6. _____ living in nature

7. _____ a lot of trees covering a large area

8. _____ to see or find for the first time

D Work with a partner. Discuss these questions.

1. What wild animals or natural places do you want to protect? Explain your reasons.
2. Do you have any goals for the future? What are they? When do you plan to reach them?
3. What are some possible dangers of exploring wild places?

E Here are some possible rewards for taking risks. According to your opinion, rank them from 1 (most important) to 5 (least important).

Rank	Reward for Taking a Risk
	to have fun or feel excitement
	to see beauty
	to teach others
	to learn about new things
	to protect human or animal life

F Work in a small group. Discuss your answers to exercise E. Do you agree on the order? Why or why not? Explain.

Photographer Joel Sartore takes a photograph of a baby caiman in Madidi National Park, Brazil.

Listening A Conversation about Emma Stokes

BEFORE LISTENING

PREVIEWING **A** Look at the photos and read the information. Discuss your answers to the questions with a partner.

1. Which country are the lowland gorillas in? _____
   Which continent? _____

2. What does *endangered* or *at risk* mean? _____

3. What does Emma Stokes hope to do? _____

▼ A lowland gorilla family in tall grass, Mbeli Bai, Nouabale-Ndoki National Park, Republic of the Congo

> **MEET EMMA STOKES** Emma Stokes is a conservationist and wildlife researcher. This means she works to protect wild animals and the places where they live. She does this by working with governments and private companies to create goals that are good for everyone.

WHILE LISTENING

B 🎧 2.9 Listen to the conversation. Then choose the correct answer to complete the main ideas.

LISTENING FOR MAIN IDEAS

1. Emma Stokes helps protect _____ .
   a. all animals
   b. endangered animals
   c. forests

2. Her job is risky because _____ .
   a. she isn't healthy
   b. some people are angry
   c. wild animals can hurt you

3. Emma and her team were in danger because of a group of _____ in their camp.
   a. gorillas
   b. tigers
   c. elephants

4. She discovered a large number of _____ .
   a. gorillas
   b. tigers
   c. elephants

C 🎧 2.9 Listen again. Check (✓) the details you hear. Then compare your answers with a partner.

LISTENING FOR DETAILS

1. ☐ Rebecca is watching a video.

2. ☐ Emma protects elephants.

3. ☐ Emma works to protect gorillas.

4. ☐ Elephants walked through Emma's camp.

5. ☐ Emma and her team found 125 gorillas.

6. ☐ The gorillas were in a popular tourist site.

7. ☐ The number of gorillas was surprising.

8. ☐ The gorilla population is not in danger now.

D 🎧 2.9 Listen again. Correct the incorrect details in exercise C. Add notes to the correct details. Note any other information you hear.

AFTER LISTENING

NOTE-TAKING SKILL Reviewing Your Notes

Reviewing your notes soon after you listen can help you remember and learn material more effectively.

- Read your notes within a day. Add any information that you remember. Add a question mark (?) if you need more information and follow up later.
- Cross out information that is not important. Keep your focus on the important information (main ideas and details).
- Compare your notes with a classmate's notes. Add any information you missed. Ask your teacher to explain any information that is difficult.

E Review your notes in exercise C and make any corrections. Then compare your notes with a partner. Add or fix anything that isn't clear.

NOTE TAKING

B Speaking

GRAMMAR FOR SPEAKING Simple Past

We use the simple past to talk about completed actions or ideas. The same form of the verb is used for all subjects (*I, you, he/she/it, we, you, they*).

- Regular verbs: add *-d/-ed* (*walk**ed**, hik**ed**, guid**ed**, climb**ed***).
- Irregular verbs: learn the different past forms (*run-**ran**; swim-**swam**; think-**thought***).

Affirmative	Negative
We **hiked** up the mountain last Saturday.	We **didn't hike** down until Sunday.
John **fell** and **broke** his arm.	He **didn't break** his leg.

Yes/No Questions	Answers
Did you **camp** on top of the mountain?	Yes, we **did**. / No, we **didn't**.
Did you **see** any animals?	Yes, I **did**. / No, I **didn't**.

Irregular Verbs in the Past

Base Form	Simple Past	Base Form	Simple Past
be	was/were	go	went
do	did	have	had
feel	felt	hear	heard
find	found	know	knew
get	got	wake up	woke up

A 🎧 2.10 Complete the excerpt from the conversation on page 97 with the simple past form of a verb in the box. Then listen to check your answers.

discover	find	go	know
feel	get	hear	wake up

Rebecca: … In the middle of the night, she _____ because she _____
1   2
screaming and _____ heavy footsteps. The ground was moving under her.
3
Marcus: Yikes!

Rebecca: Yeah, they _____ it, but they were right in the middle of an
4
elephant path.

Marcus: That's scary! Was she OK?

Rebecca: Yes, luckily everyone _____ out of the way in time.
5
Marcus: Why _____ she _____ there?
6   6
Rebecca: She _____ to count the number of gorillas. Her goal was to protect
7
them.

Marcus: _____ she _____ any?
8   8
Rebecca: Yes, she actually _____ 125,000. No one _____ they were
9   10
there.

PRONUNCIATION Simple Past -ed Endings

🎧 **2.11** The -d/-ed at the end of regular simple past verbs has three different sounds. The pronunciation depends on the final sound of the verb. Listen.

The -d/-ed ending sounds like:

- /əd/ (or /ɪd/) after verbs ending with /t, d/. This forms a new syllable.
  need**ed**, count**ed**, wait**ed**

- /t/ after voiceless consonants /f, k, p, s, ʃ, tʃ/.
  surf**ed**, hik**ed**, hopp**ed**, kiss**ed**, wash**ed**, watch**ed**

- /d/ after voiced consonants /b, g, ð, ʒ, dʒ, l, m, n, ŋ, r, v, z/ and all vowels.
  bath**ed**, judg**ed**, offer**ed**, solv**ed**, play**ed**

B 🎧 **2.12** Work with a partner. Take turns saying the simple past form of each word. Write the word in the correct column. Then listen and check your answers.

camp	discover	help	protect	risk
die	guide	jump	receive	vote

/əd/ or /ɪd/	/t/	/d/
	camped	

C Work with a partner. Tell about one or two dangers you faced in your life. Use the simple past.

PERSONALIZING

> *One day, in my back yard, I saw a large snake. It was scary. It looked dangerous. I went to get a camera, but when I returned, it wasn't there anymore.*

Western diamondback rattlesnake, a dangerous snake found in the western United States and Mexico, Coastal Bend, Texas, USA

FINAL TASK Telling a Story

> You will tell a story about a time you took a risk. You will use the simple past and give examples when necessary.

BRAINSTORMING **A** In your notebook, brainstorm times in your life when you took a risk. Choose one of them. Write it and tell why you took the risk.

Risk: _____

Why you took the risk: _____

ORGANIZING IDEAS **B** Complete the chart with information about your risk from exercise A. Then take turns asking and answering questions with a partner.

When	
Where	
Who	
What happened?	
How did you feel?	

PRESENTATION SKILL Asking for Questions

Leave time at the end of your talk and maybe at important places during your talk to let your listeners ask questions. Use these phrases.

Are there any questions?

I'd be happy to answer any questions.

PRESENTING **C** Form a group with another pair. Present your story to your group. Remember to give examples, use the simple past, and ask for questions at the end.

REFLECTION

1. Why does reviewing your notes help you remember more?

_____

_____

2. Who in your life takes the most risks? How do they do it? Do you think the rewards are worth the risk? Why or why not?

_____

_____

3. Here are the words from the unit. Check (✓) the ones you can use.

☐ adventure   ☐ die   ☐ protect

☐ body   ☐ difficult   ☐ solve

☐ climb   ☐ discover   ☐ vote

☐ count   ☐ forest   ☐ wild

☐ danger   ☐ goal AWL

☐ decrease   ☐ mind

TAKING ACTION 6

Earth, we believe, is the only planet with life on it. Humans, together with air, water, land, and other life, create our beautiful and constantly changing world.

ACADEMIC SKILLS

LISTENING	Listening for Emotion
	Using Symbols and Abbreviations
SPEAKING	Giving Sources of Information
	Be Going To (Gonna)
CRITICAL THINKING	Understanding Bias

THINK AND DISCUSS

1 How does the Earth change over time?
2 What are some ways humans create changes to the Earth?
3 What kinds of things do people do to protect the Earth? Do they work? Explain.

EXPLORE THE THEME

Look at the photo and read the information. Then discuss the questions.

1. How is trash in our oceans a problem? Explain.
2. What does the information in the graph tell you? Which objects are worse for the environment? Explain.
3. Do you think people can help solve the problem of trash in our oceans? How?

THE TRUTH ABOUT TRASH

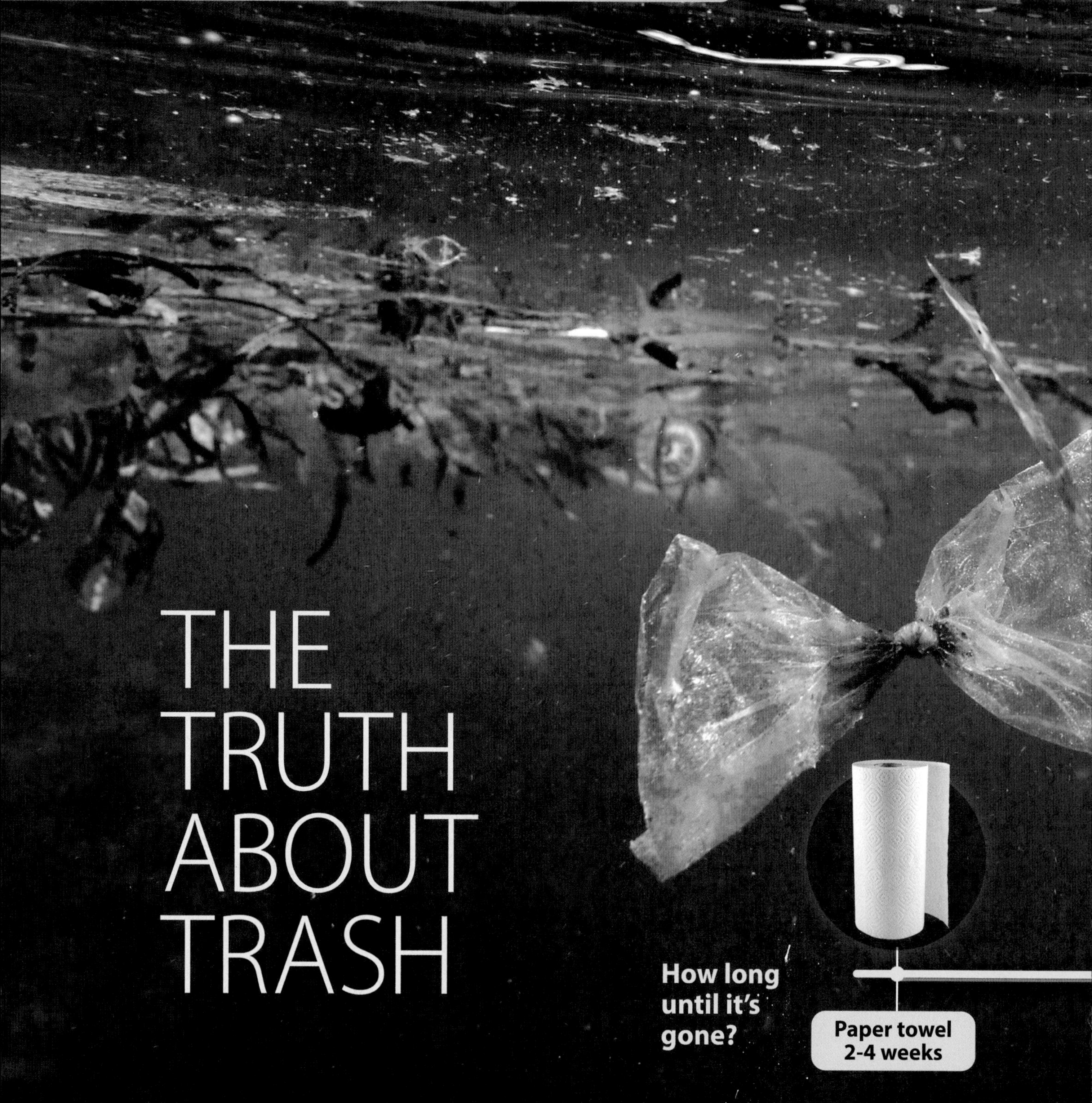
How long until it's gone?
Paper towel 2-4 weeks

Years

500

400

300

200

100

0

Banana peel
2-5 weeks

Plastic bag
10-20 years

Styrofoam cup
50+ years

Plastic bottle
450 years

Vocabulary

A 🎧 **2.13** Listen and check (✓) the words and phrases you already know.

☐ according to (*prep*) ☐ especially (*adv*) ☐ reduce (*v*) ☐ throw away (*v*)
☐ believe (*v*) ☐ habits (*n*) ☐ research (*n*) ☐ worst (*adj*)

MEANING FROM
CONTEXT

B 🎧 **2.14** Read and listen to the information. Notice each word or phrase in **blue** and think about its meaning.

Easy Ways You Can Use Less Plastic

According to many scientists, plastic trash is a big problem. Many say it is the **worst** problem in our world today. Follow these five easy tips to change your everyday **habits** with trash.

Tip 1

Stop buying water in plastic bottles. Many people **believe** bottled water is better than water from your kitchen sink, but **research** shows that bottled water is often not safer.

Tip 2

Don't use and then **throw away** plastic utensils. Take a fork, knife, spoon, and/or chopsticks with you.

Tip 3

Take a bag with you to the store. Say "no" to paper and plastic bags, **especially** plastic ones.

Tip 4

Buy your food in glass jars. Save the jars and reuse them.

Tip 5

Reduce the number of things you buy and throw away soon after.

C Write the correct word from exercise A next to its definition.

1. _____ opposite of *best*

2. _____ more than usual

3. _____ information about something that a scientist carefully studied

4. _____ things we do regularly or every day

5. _____ in the words of

6. _____ to think something is true

7. _____ to make something smaller in number or size

8. _____ to put something you no longer want in a trash can

VOCABULARY SKILL Prefixes: *re-* and *un-*

A prefix is one or more letters that come at the beginning of certain words. Some common prefixes are *re-* (*again* or *back*) and *un-* (*not*). Learning them will help you form new words or understand words you hear.

Word	Prefix	Part of Speech	Meaning
redo	re-	verb	to do again
reuse	re-	verb	to use again
undo	un-	verb	to change or release
unlike	un-	adjective	not like others, different
unusual	un-	adjective	not usual

D Read the statements. Add the prefix *re-* or *un-* to complete each statement.

1. There are many ways you can _____use a plastic shopping bag.

2. She hurt her leg. She's _____able to help clean the beach this weekend.

3. Our oceans are _____safe for sea animals.

4. I don't understand everything about the topic. I need to _____read the information.

5. I'm _____satisfied with your work. You need to _____do it.

6. My essay wasn't good. I need to _____write it before Monday.

7. This idea is great. It's _____like any other!

8. Did you _____cycle the bottles?

E Look back at the tips in exercise B. Which do you do? Which can you do in the future? Tell a partner or small group. Give examples where possible.   PERSONALIZING

> I take a bag with me to the store most of the time. I keep a couple in my car. I'm going to buy some forks and spoons that I can carry with me and reuse. I'd like to stop using so much plastic.

A Listening   Student Podcast: Oceans of Plastic

BEFORE LISTENING

PRIOR KNOWLEDGE **A** Look at the map and photo. Read the title of the podcast. What do you already know about the topic? Tell a partner.

PREDICTING **B** Choose the answer you think is correct to complete each main idea from the podcast.

1. Plastic in the Pacific Ocean (is / isn't) a major problem.
2. People (are /aren't) responsible for the plastic in the ocean.
3. The problem (is / isn't) getting better each year.
4. Plastic in the ocean (hurts / doesn't hurt) sea animals.
5. Plastic in the ocean (hurts / doesn't hurt) humans.

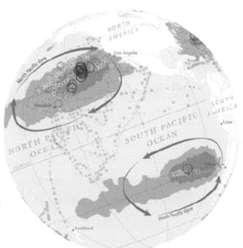

▲ **Huge amounts of plastic trash float in the world's oceans.**

WHILE LISTENING

LISTENING FOR MAIN IDEAS **C** 🎧 2.15 ▶ 1.10 Listen to the podcast. Check your answers to exercise B. Were your predictions correct?

LISTENING FOR DETAILS **D** 🎧 2.15 Listen to the podcast again. Choose **T** for *True* or **F** for *False*. Compare your answers with a partner. Then correct the false answers.

1. There is a garbage patch, or an "island" of trash, in the ~~Atlantic~~ *Pacific* Ocean.	**T**	**(F)**
2. The speaker believes that plastic is the worst type of trash.	**T**	**F**
3. Over 90 percent of the seabirds in the world have eaten plastic.	**T**	**F**
4. Over 10,000 other sea animals die each year because of plastic trash.	**T**	**F**
5. Many sea animals eat plastic in the water.	**T**	**F**
6. The speaker believes cleaning the oceans is the only solution.	**T**	**F**

Sea turtle eating a plastic bag that looks like a jellyfish

NOTE-TAKING SKILL Using Symbols and Abbreviations

We use symbols or abbreviate (shorten) words to write more quickly and note more points from a talk or lecture. Here are some common examples.

Symbol/ abbreviation	Meaning	Example
=	*equals* or *is/are*	plastic = worst trash
< or >	less/fewer or more than	> $40,000 but < $50,000
%	percent	50% = a half (1/2)
mil./bil.	million/billion	65 mil./bil. years old

E [2.16] Listen to the *Did You Know* part of the podcast. Write a symbol or abbreviation from the box above to complete the student's notes correctly.   NOTE TAKING

Facts about Plastic

- plastic in last 10 yrs ___ 1900s
- 50___ plastic used, use 1 time
- average American plastic trash ___ 185 pounds a year
- Americans throw away 35 _____ water bottles a year
- people in world use ___ 1 _____ plastic bags a minute

LISTENING SKILL Listening for Emotion

People's faces often change according to how they feel. A smile often means a person is happy. The way people speak can also change according to how they feel. For example, when speakers feel

- passionate/angry, they put more stress on words; they may pause after each word to be sure every word is clear.
- sad/unhappy, they may be quieter, and the stressed syllables may not be as strong.

F [2.17] How does each speaker feel? Listen and choose the correct emotion.

1. The problem is getting worse every year.   a. passionate   b. sad
2. The sea turtle at the animal hospital died.   a. passionate   b. sad
3. The time to reduce plastic is now.   a. passionate   b. sad
4. We must change our habits.   a. passionate   b. sad
5. I just watched a video about seabirds.   a. passionate   b. sad

AFTER LISTENING

G Work with a partner. Choose three statements from this lesson and say them with emotion. Your partner guesses which emotion you are expressing.

A: *There is an **is**land of **trash** in the Pacific **O**cean!*
B: *You are angry!*

A Speaking

> **GRAMMAR FOR SPEAKING** Future with *Be Going To*
>
> We use the phrase *be (not) going to* + a base verb:
>
> - to make predictions about the future.
>   *I think people **are going to get** sicker. We**'re going to be** sorry.*
>
> - to discuss planned future activities or intentions.
>   *I**'m going to help** clean the beach. I**'m not going to buy** water in a bottle again.*
>
> | Affirmative | Negative |
> |---|---|
> | The test **is going to be** hard. | The test **isn't going to be** easy. |
> | I**'m going to study** all weekend. | I**'m not going to watch** TV. |
>
> | Questions | Answers |
> |---|---|
> | **Are** you **going to stop** using plastic? | Yes, I **am**. / No, I**'m not**. |
> | When **is** he **going to arrive**? | He**'s going to arrive** at about 5:00 p.m. |

A Complete the predictions or plans with the affirmative or negative form of *be going to*. Use your own beliefs or predictions. Then write a prediction or plan of your own.

1. We _____ find a solution to the problem of plastic trash.

2. People _____ stop buying bottled water.

3. My country _____ create laws and programs to reduce trash.

4. In the future, people _____ live on other planets, such as Mars.

5. I _____ change my habits.

6. Your prediction/plan: _____

   _____

> **PRONUNCIATION** *Be Going To (Gonna)*
>
> 🎧 **2.18** We often reduce unstressed words or phrases when we speak. For *going to*, we often say *gonna*. You do not need to use reduced forms, but practicing and listening to them will help you communicate more effectively. Listen to the examples.
>
> A: *Hey.* **Are** you **going to speak** at the town meeting?
> B: *No, but I**'m going to** be there.*

B Work with a partner. Share your answers from exercise A. Reduce *going to* to *gonna*.

> ❯ *I predict that <u>we're going to find a solution to the problem of plastic trash.</u>*

C 🎧 **2.19** Listen to Emily speak at a meeting of the *Clean and Green* project. Check (✓) each action when you hear the speaker say it.

1. _____ read the plans we discussed at last month's meeting

2. _____ not plant 100 trees this year

3. _____ plant 200 trees this year

4. _____ talk about a project in Nanjing, China

5. _____ have tall buildings with trees and plants on them

6. _____ discuss a project in Ljubljana, Slovenia

7. _____ pick up any old coffee, fruits, and vegetables

8. _____ teach a class about growing your own food

9. _____ have *Clean the River* events

10. _____ organize the *Clean the River* events

D 🎧 **2.19** Listen again and write the number of the action in exercise C next to the person or group that is going to do it. Then tell your partner your answers. Use *gonna*.

CRITICAL THINKING: CATEGORIZING

> *Emily is going to read the plans discussed at last month's meeting.*

1. Emily _1._____

2. The group _____

3. Tim _____

4. Nanjing, China _____

5. Vladimir _____

6. Kumiko _____

Vertical forest; view from below

SPEAKING SKILL Giving Sources of Information

When you are supporting your beliefs or ideas, you often need to include information from a variety of sources such as articles, books, Internet sites, diagrams, charts, or a survey. Here are common phrases we use when giving sources of information.

> **According to** the diagram, it takes two to four weeks for a paper towel to break down.
> The podcast **stated that** people use 1 million plastic bags each minute.
> Our survey **found that** half of the students buy a bottled drink every day.
> Research **shows that** 50% of the plastic we use is for one-time use.

E Look back for this information in the lesson. Then with your partner, take turns giving the source and restating the information.

Example: It takes about 450 years for a plastic bottle to break down. (page 102–103)

> *The diagram shows that it takes about 450 years for a plastic bottle to break down.*

1. It takes over 50 years for a Styrofoam cup to break down. (page 102–103)
2. Americans throw away 35 billion water bottles each year. (page 107)
3. One way to reduce plastic is to take a bag with you to the store. (page 104)
4. Nanjing, China, has an interesting project to help clean the air. (page 109)

PERSONALIZING **F** Work in a group of four. Complete column 1 with your own answers and complete columns 2–4 with your group members' answers. Put a check (✓) for *yes* or an X for *no*.

GREEN HABITS

Question	1	2	3	4
1. Do you usually take a bag with you to the store?				
2. Do you buy one or more bottles of water each week?				
3. Do you want to change some of your habits or the habits of people you know?				
4. Do you know about projects in your town that help the environment?				
5. Do you think each country needs to do more to help the environment?				

CRITICAL THINKING: ANALYZING RESULTS **G** In your group, analyze the information from your survey in exercise F. Then share the results with your class. Each group member takes a turn sharing a result or two.

> *According to our survey, three of us usually take a bag to the store.*

LESSON TASK Presenting a Project Plan

A Work in a small group. Complete these steps.

BRAINSTORMING

1. Research problems in your town or area. Make a list in your notebook. The problems can be about trash or another problem in your town.

    Example: Littering (trash on streets, in rivers, lakes, public parks)

2. Choose one of the problems and discuss possible ways you can help as a group.

    Example: Plan a Clean Our Streets day each month. Ask other students to help.

B Discuss and take notes in your notebook about each part of your presentation. Decide who will present which part.

ORGANIZING IDEAS

1. What is the problem? Give sources for any information about the problem.

2. What is your group going to do to help solve the problem? What are the steps?

3. When are you going to do it? How are you going to tell people about it? Who in your group is going to do what?

C Each group member should prepare one part of the presentation. Use the example as a guide. Give sources for any information and practice the reduced form of *going to*.

PRESENTING

> **Li:** *According to an article last month in the* Daily Post, *there's a problem with trash in City Park. There are some volunteer organizations, but they all say they need more help, especially during spring and summer.*
>
> **Javier:** *Our group is going to plan a day of action in May. We're going to clean City Park. According to the city website, they provide gloves and bags.*
>
> **Massa:** *Li is going to create a poster to tell people about the day of action. We're hoping to get 40–50 students. Javier is going to visit City Hall and ask for some gloves and bags. I'm going to visit some local restaurants to see if they'll give us a free dinner. We plan to give students who collect the most trash a prize.*

Volunteers pick up plastic bottles in a park.

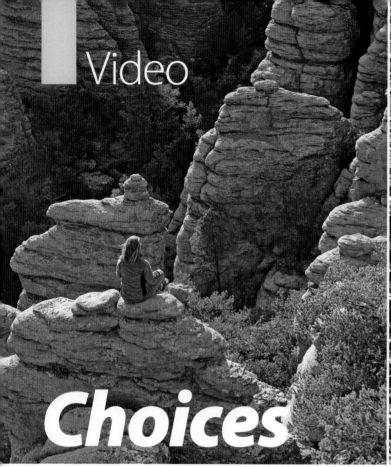

Video

Choices

▲ (left) Chiricahua
National Monument
in Chiricahua
Mountains, Arizona,
USA

▲ (right) Crowded
housing
development in
Phoenix, Arizona,
USA

BEFORE VIEWING

A Look at the photos and read the captions. Discuss your answers to these questions with your class.

1. What is the first photo of? What is the second photo of?
2. What does the first photo say to you about Arizona? The second?
3. Which photo do you think is better? Explain.

B Match each word from the video with its definition. Use your dictionary to help you.

choice	generation	legacy	profound
extraordinary	image	memories	wonder

1. _____ (n) something we leave for future people to have or own

2. _____ (n) a picture or a view

3. _____ (n) people born around the same time

4. _____ (n) what one remembers about a past event or time

5. _____ (adj) very strong in feeling or emotion

6. _____ (adj) amazing; uncommon or unusual

7. _____ (v) to express interest in knowing something

8. _____ (n) the power or ability to choose

WHILE VIEWING

C ▶ `1.11` Watch Parts 1 and 2 of the video. In the *Images* column, take notes on the images you see. Then compare your notes with a partner.

Part	Images	Feelings about the United States
1	girl on rock pretty road	
2		

D How did you feel about the United States after seeing the images in Part 1? In Part 2? Discuss your ideas with your partner and write your ideas in the *Feelings* column above.

AFTER VIEWING

> **CRITICAL THINKING**   Understanding Bias
>
> *Bias* is believing that some people or ideas are better or worse without thinking about the facts. Many sources (reports, news, diagrams, etc.) may have a bias. They may use photos or stories to create the story they want. It's important to be aware of bias and always look for a variety of sources when thinking about any issue.

E Work in a small group. Discuss these questions.

1. How did the photos in the video change your thoughts or feelings in Part 1 and Part 2?

2. How is the woman's voice or emotion different in Part 1 and Part 2? Did this change your thoughts or feelings?

3. Give one example of bias in the world.

B Vocabulary

A 🎧 **2.20** Listen and check (✓) the words you already know. Then discuss their meaning with a partner. Check the dictionary for any you are not sure about.

☐ behavior (*n*)   ☐ garden (*n*)   ☐ increase (*v*)   ☐ prisons (*n*)
☐ criminals (*n*)   ☐ guest (*n*)   ☐ pretty (*adv*)   ☐ purpose (*n*)

MEANING FROM
CONTEXT

B 🎧 **2.21** Look at the photo and read the caption. What do you think the title *Nature Behind Bars* means? Complete the information with the words in exercise A. Then listen and check your answers.

▶ **A prisoner cares for an injured owl.**

NATURE BEHIND BARS

Several universities around the country have projects in nearby _____.
The aim is to help the prisoners learn about nature. The projects send _____ [2]
speakers, offer classes, or do some type of research. For example, some have started
a _____ [3] where prisoners can grow food and take notes on different plants
and give their notes to scientists. Other projects involve animals. Research shows that
working with nature can _____ [4] a person's level of happiness.

Further, the work gives prisoners a _____ [5]. They do not usually have
much to do in prison, and life can be _____ [6] boring. Working on the projects
teaches them about gardening and animal _____ [7].

Very dangerous _____ [8] cannot usually do these activities. However, nature
can still help. To test her ideas, one researcher put photos of nature (such as trees and
plants) in their prison cells.* She wanted to see if it made them happier. The results
show that even photos of nature can help people.

*cells: the small rooms in a prison where prisoners live

C Match each word from exercise A with its definition.

1. _____ behavior   a. a little less than "very"

2. _____ criminals   b. to make bigger or to make more of

3. _____ garden   c. the way somone acts

4. _____ guest   d. a reason

5. _____ increase   e. a visitor

6. _____ pretty   f. people who do something wrong such as stealing

7. _____ prisons   g. the places where criminals have to go

8. _____ purpose   h. a place where you grow vegetables, flowers, or other plants

D Complete the sentences. Choose the correct form of the word. (See page 85 and 105 for a review of suffixes and prefixes.)

1. A (prisoner / prisoning) helped the researcher with the owl.

2. Sometimes I (reuse / using) plastic bags from the store to carry my lunch to school. I (repurpose / unpurpose) them whenever I can.

3. I love (gardener / gardening). I grew my first tomatoes this summer.

4. My friend, Jana, is a (gardener / gardening). She grows flowers.

E Work with a partner. Discuss the questions.

CRITICAL THINKING: EVALUATING

1. Do you think it is good to help criminals living in prisons? Why or why not?

2. Do you think prisoners should have work or some other purpose? Explain.

3. How can a garden be useful in a prison?

Prisoners working in a garden

LETTUCE

EGG PLANT

B Listening   A Conversation about Nalini Nadkarni

BEFORE LISTENING

PREVIEWING **A** Read the information about National Geographic Explorer Nalini Nadkarni. What types of projects do you think she does with musicians and prisoners?

MEET NALINI NADKARNI Nalini Nadkarni is an American ecologist who studies trees. She studies the importance of trees to all life. She also works in creative ways to teach all people about the importance of nature and conservation.* She's worked with musicians, fashion designers, prisoners, and others.

*conservation: the protection of nature (animals, plants, and so on)

WHILE LISTENING

LISTENING FOR MAIN IDEAS **B** 🎧 2.22 Listen to the conversation. Check (✓) the two main ideas of the conversation.

_____ Jamal and Claudi both study science.

_____ Jamal and Claudi are both interested in going to a talk Friday evening.

_____ Nalini Nadkarni works with trees in forests.

_____ Nalini Nadkarni works to increase people's interest in nature.

LISTENING FOR DETAILS **C** 🎧 2.22 Listen again. Choose the correct answers.

1. Nalini Nadkarni studies _____.
   a. trees   b. prison fights   c. rap musicians

2. Nadkarni did a project with a rap musician and _____.
   a. dancers   b. prisoners   c. city kids

3. Nadkarni is speaking tonight about her work _____.
   a. with children   b. in forests   c. in prisons

4. Her research showed that seeing _____ decreased the number of fights.
   a. photos of trees   b. gardens   c. research

5. Prisoners helped Nadkarni with her _____.
   a. class   b. research   c. photos

Dr. Nadkarni teaches about trees at Stafford Creek Corrections Center.

AFTER LISTENING

D With a partner, discuss two students' statements about prisoners. Do they show bias? Give reasons. Which do you agree with more? Explain.

CRITICAL THINKING: UNDERSTANDING BIAS

Student 1: *Prisoners don't have much to do all day, so the projects are good for them. People need something to do.*

Student 2: *I don't think prisoners should have these special projects. They are criminals.*

E Look back at the information in Lesson A about reducing trash, plastic in the oceans, and the *Clean and Green* project. Then in a small group, discuss these questions.

CRITICAL THINKING: SYNTHESIZING

1. How is the information in Lesson A similar to the ideas discussed in this lesson? How is it different?

2. Which information in Lessons A and B did you find most surprising? Explain.

B Speaking

GRAMMAR FOR SPEAKING Future with *Will*

We use *will* + a base verb:

- to make predictions.
  *I think humans **will learn** to care for the environment.*

- to talk about unplanned actions.
  A: *I don't want to go alone. Will you come with me?*
  B: *Sure, I'**ll go** with you.*

Contractions (*'ll* or *won't*) are common in speaking.

Affirmative	Negative
The lecture **will be** interesting.	The lecture **won't last** more than an hour.
The project **will take** years.	The project **won't happen** this year.

Questions	Answers
Will you **help** teach the kids?	Yes, I **will**. / No, I **won't**.
When **will** the problem **end**?	It'**ll end** when we do something about it.

A Change the statements to predictions. Use *will* or *won't*. Write answers according to what you believe.

1. English is the global language of business.

   I predict ___English won't be the global language of business___ in the future.

2. The prisoners care about nature.

   I predict _____ when they get out of prison.

3. Many prisons have similar projects.

   I predict _____ in the future.

4. Some prisoners work in gardens.

   I predict _____ in the future.

5. College students work with the prison project.

   I predict _____ after they graduate.

6. Your prediction _____

B Work with a partner. Take turns asking about your partner's predictions in exercise A and telling about your own predictions. Discuss predictions you don't agree on.

A: *Will English be the global language of business in the future?*
B: *No, I predict that English won't be the global language of business in the future.*

When we are working in a group, we often offer to do something or help someone. For example, someone may need help with a project, and others will offer to help.

A: *Who wants to research photos for our project?*

B: *I'll do it.*

A: *Great, thanks.*

A: *Who'll bring drinks?*

B: *Johan said he'll bring water. I'll get some juice.*

A: *Perfect. Thanks, and remember—no plastic bottles!*

C Read the situations. With a partner, role play the situations. Include an offer to help.

A: *My car broke down. I can't get to class!*

B: *I'll take you.*

1. A friend needs a ride to school.

2. A group member needs someone to read his or her essay.

3. Your professor asks for someone to help at the prison, either in the garden or with the small animals.

FINAL TASK   Presenting a Project Using Images

You will find photos or other images to go with your group's project from lesson A on page 111. You will present the project individually to your group, but this time you will use photos, maps, a chart, or other images.

A Join your group from the Lesson Task on page 111 (or join any group if you were not in class). Discuss the ideas you presented and possible images that you can use. Take notes.

BRAINSTORMING

B For homework, each group member looks for photos, charts, or other visual information. In class, present your ideas to your group.

In some presentations, photos can help your listeners understand your ideas better. Here are some tips for using photos.

• Choose photos that are large and clear enough to see.
• Use photos that help explain new or different ideas when you can.
• Introduce photos with phrases such as: *As you can see in this photo,…; Here you can see… ; In this photo, …; Take a look at….*

C As a group, choose the best photos and images from your group's research. Then plan your presentation using a chart like the one below.

Presentation	Image
According to an article last month in the Daily News, there is a problem with trash in City Park. As you can see in this photo of the park, it is a big problem. ...	
Our group is going to plan a day of action in May. We're going to clean City Park. In this photo, a local group is cleaning another park using city help. ...	
Li is going to create a poster to tell people about the day of action. Take a look at one of her great designs. ...	

PRESENTING **D** Give your presentation again with photos and images. Add language as needed to introduce your photos.

REFLECTION

1. In your language or others you know, how do speakers express emotion? Is it similar to English or different? Explain.

   _____

   _____

2. What are some projects to help the environment in your country? Give an example.

   _____

   _____

3. Here are the vocabulary words from the unit. Check (✓) the ones you can use.

   ☐ according to   ☐ guest   ☐ reduce

   ☐ behavior   ☐ habit   ☐ research **AWL**

   ☐ believe   ☐ increase   ☐ throw away

   ☐ criminal   ☐ pretty   ☐ worst

   ☐ especially   ☐ prison

   ☐ garden   ☐ purpose

LOST AND FOUND 7

King Tutankhamun's burial mask with a looter's gloved hand, Cairo, Egypt

THINK AND DISCUSS

1 Look at this photo. What do you see?
2 The photo caption mentions a "looter's gloved hand." What do you think looters do? Why?
3 What do you think this unit will be about?

121

Look at the map and the timeline and read the information. Then discuss the questions.

1. Who was Ramses I? When did he lead Egypt? When did he die?
2. What happened to Ramses I's mummy? How long was it in each place?
3. Where is Ramses I now? Do you think museum in Atlanta did the right thing? Why?

FINDERS KEEPERS?

Ramses I, one of ancient Egypt's most important leaders ruled during this time.

Ramses I died and was buried in the Valley of the Kings.

1293-1290 B.C.   1290 B.C.

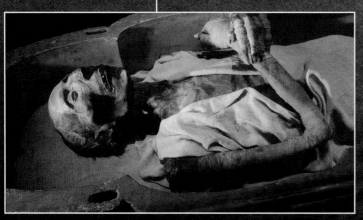

Mummy of Ramses I

A tomb after looters visted

Ramses I's Long Trip Home

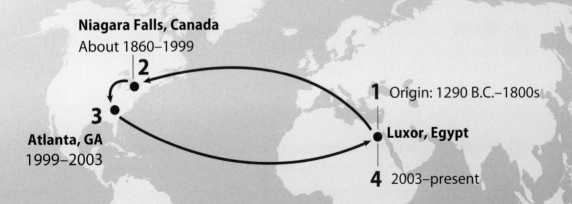

Niagara Falls, Canada
About 1860–1999

2

3

Atlanta, GA
1999–2003

1 Origin: 1290 B.C.–1800s

Luxor, Egypt

4 2003–present

Looters stole the mummy of Ramses I. Soon after, James Douglas, a Canadian, bought a mummy for the Niagara Falls Museum in Canada.

A museum in Atlanta bought the mummy from the Niagara Falls Museum.

Researchers in Atlanta discovered that the mummy was Ramses I, so they returned it to Egypt; Ramses I is now back home.

Mid-1800s

1999

2003-present

Michael C. Carlos Museum in Atlanta, Georgia, USA

Tomb of Ramses I in Valley of the Kings, Luxor West Bank, Egypt

A Vocabulary

A 🎧 **2.23** Listen and check the words you already know.

☐ find (*v*)   ☐ hide (*v*)   ☐ missing (*adj*)   ☐ objects (*n*)

☐ gold (*n*)   ☐ jewels (*n*)   ☐ mystery (*n*)   ☐ search (*v*)

MEANING FROM CONTEXT

B 🎧 **2.24** Look at the photo and read the caption. Then read and listen to the information. Notice each word in **blue** and think about its meaning.

LOST TREASURE: FABERGÉ EGGS

In cultures around the world, an egg is a symbol that means new life, birth, or springtime. For thousands of years, people all over the world have colored or decorated eggs.

In 1885, Alexander III, the Tsar (or King) of Russia, wanted to give his wife a special gift, so he asked the famous artist Peter Carl Fabergé to make an egg with **gold** and **jewels**. His wife loved the egg so much that he gave her a new one every year. They had 50 of these beautiful **objects** when the Tsar and his family were killed during the Russian Revolution*, but at some point, they disappeared. Did someone take the eggs? Did the Tsar **hide** them? Today, 43 of the eggs were found and are in museums around the world, but there are still 7 **missing** eggs. Each egg is probably worth millions of dollars today! Nobody knows where these eggs are, but many **search** for them. It's a complete **mystery**. Who will be the first person to **find** one?

*Russian Revolution: In 1917, the people of Russia fought against Tsar Nicolas II and the government.

This Fabergé egg made in 1900 has 1,618 rose-cut diamonds. The little elephant inside the egg can walk and move its trunk.

C Match each word with its definition.

1. _____ hide
2. _____ mystery
3. _____ search
4. _____ gold
5. _____ jewels
6. _____ find
7. _____ objects
8. _____ missing

a. expensive stones
b. things that you can see or touch
c. something that is difficult to explain
d. not there; no one can find it
e. to discover something
f. to look for
g. to put something where no one can see it
h. a yellow metal that is worth a lot of money

VOCABULARY SKILL Using a Dictionary to Find a Word Form

Many words have different forms (noun, verb, adjective, adverb). You can increase your vocabulary by knowing the different forms of words you already know. To help you do this, use a dictionary to find different word forms and keep a log or list in your notebook. Here are some words with both noun and adjective forms.

Noun	Adjective
beauty	*beautiful*
storm	*stormy*
possibility	*possible*

D Use a dictionary and write the adjective forms of the nouns in the chart.

Noun	Adjective
1. sand	
2. gold	
3. mystery	
4. luck	
5. color	
6. power	
7. magic	
8. peace	

E Discuss the questions with a partner.

PERSONALIZING

1. Do you have an object that you feel is special? What is it? Where is it?

2. What do you do if you find something that is not yours in a restaurant or store? How about in a public place like a park or the beach?

3. Do you like mysteries (books, movies, TV shows, or video games)? Explain. If yes, tell about a favorite one.

A Listening Interview with a Treasure Hunter

BEFORE LISTENING

PREDICTING **A** You are going to hear an interview with a treasure hunter. Choose the two ideas you think you will hear in the interview.

1. _____ People pay to look for treasure.

2. _____ Searching for treasure can be dangerous.

3. _____ A man hides a treasure for anyone to find.

4. _____ People get rich because of the treasure they find.

5. _____ People like the search just as much as the treasure.

6. _____ People get angry when they can't find a treasure.

WHILE LISTENING

LISTENING FOR MAIN IDEAS **B** 🎧 2.25 Listen and check your predictions from exercise A. Write the number of the idea from exercise A in the order you hear it in the interview. Listen again if necessary.

Ist main idea: _____

2nd main idea: _____

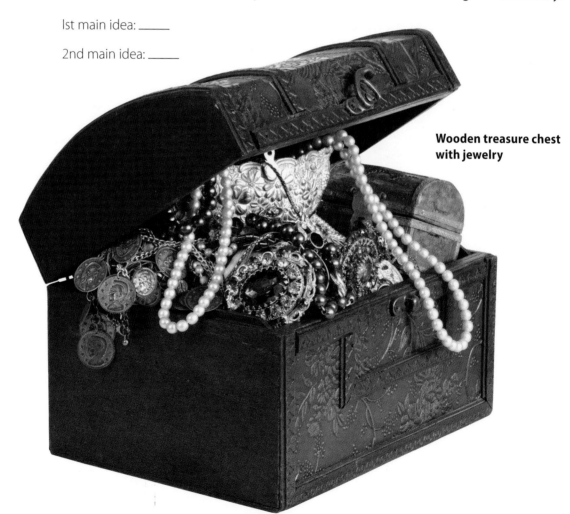

Wooden treasure chest with jewelry

We use the word *because* to give a reason. To find out the reason for something, listen for the words *why* and *because* and the information that follows.

A: Why do people like to search for treasure?
*B: People like to search for treasure **because** <u>it is exciting</u>.*

C 🎧 2.25 Listen again to the interview. Complete the chart with the reasons that answer each question. Share your answers with the class.

Question	Reasons
Why do people like to search for treasure?	1. _____ 2. _____
Why did Forrest Fenn hide a treasure?	3. _____ 4. _____ 5. _____
Why does the guest on the show search for treasure?	6. _____

AFTER LISTENING

D Work in a small group. Discuss the questions.

1. What do you do when an object is missing?

2. In the interview, the guest said, "The journey to the treasure is part of the fun." Do you agree? Explain.

3. Rank your reasons for searching for treasure from 1 to 4. (1 is the best reason.) Compare your answers with a partner. Discuss reasons for your rankings.

   > *I think "It's exciting to find something" is first because people love discovering things.*

   _____ It's exciting to find something.

   _____ It gets you out of the house.

   _____ You can become rich.

   _____ You can learn new things.

A Speaking

GRAMMAR FOR SPEAKING *Wh-* Questions in the Simple Past

Wh- questions ask for information and use question words (*who, what, where, when, why, how, how many*). To form a simple past *wh-* question, follow these patterns.

Wh- word + ***did*** + subject + **base verb**

Question	Answer
Why did *Forrest Fenn* **hide** *a treasure?*	*Because he wanted people to have fun.*
Where did *you* **see** *the missing object?*	*In the closet.*
Who did *he* **give** *the eggs to?*	*His wife.*
What did *you* **find** *in the box?*	*Gold and jewelry.*
When did *he* **lose** *the gold?*	*On his trip to Europe.*
How did *he* **color** *the eggs?*	*He used paint.*

Wh- word + **past form of *be***

Who was *Peter Carl Fabergé?*

Where were *the jewels?*

A Order the words to make *wh-* questions in the simple past.

1. When you were a child, (was / favorite / what / your / object) _____ _____ ?

2. As a child, (your / hide / special objects / where / you / did) _____ ?

3. (did / for / what / you / search) _____ last week?

4. When you last lost something important, (you / what / do / did) _____ _____ ?

PRONUNCIATION *Wh-* Question Intonation

🎧 **2.26** When we ask a question with *who, what, when, where, why, how,* or *how many,* the voice first rises and then falls at the end of the sentence. Listen to the examples.

Where did he hide it?

How did she find the missing objects?

When did they lose the jewels?

B Ask and answer the questions in exercise A with a partner. Be sure to use *wh-* question intonation.

A: *When you were a child, what was your favorite object?*

B: *I loved a silver cat necklace. My grandmother gave it to me.*

C Work with a partner. Ask questions to help each other recall the facts about the Fabergé eggs. Use the words in your questions.

A: *Who was Carl Fabergé?*
B: *He was a famous artist.*

1. Who / Carl Fabergé

2. When / Alexander / give / his wife / the first egg

3. How often / Alexander / give / his wife / an egg

4. How many / eggs / family / have

5. What / happen / to Alexander and his wife / during the Russian Revolution

6. What / happen / to the eggs / during the Russian Revolution

7. Where / eggs / today

8. How much / eggs / worth today

D Work with a partner. Partner A, stay on this page. Partner B, look at page 130. Follow the instructions.

1. Partner A, you need to get information about the story *Lost Ship of the Desert*. Ask Partner B questions and try to complete the chart with the answers.

    > *What is the* Lost Ship of the Desert *about?*

	Lost Ship of the Desert
What	It's about sailors from Spain. Their ship sank.
Where	
When	
How	

2. Partner A, read *Lost Treasure Ships* and answer questions for Partner B. Then ask Partner B to tell you the story.

LOST TREASURE SHIPS
In 1715, 11 Spanish treasure ships were near Florida. A storm came, and all 11 ships sank to the bottom of the ocean. People found 7 of the ships, but the treasure is still missing.

Divers near the *Mary Celestia*, a ship that sank in 1865 off the coast of Bermuda

3. Partner B, read *Lost Ship of the Desert* and answer questions for Partner A. Then ask Partner A to tell you the story.

LOST SHIP OF THE DESERT
In 1615, some sailors from Spain were on a ship in the Pacific Ocean. The ship had gold and jewels on it. Then it went down a river in California. The river became dry, and the ship went into the sand. Nobody ever found the ship.

4. Partner B, you need to get information about the story *Lost Treasure Ships*. Ask Partner A questions and try to complete the chart with the answers.

	Lost Treasure Ships
What	
Where	
When	
How	

SPEAKING SKILL Saying Years Correctly

To say a year before 2000, break the number into a pair of two-digit numbers.

1985: 19–85   **1848**: 18–48   **1621**: 16–21

Between the years 2000 and 2009, we say the number as a whole.

2001: two thousand one   **2005**: two thousand five   **2009**: two thousand nine

For the years 2010 and later, we can say it both ways.

2011: 20–11 OR two thousand eleven   **2016**: 20–16 OR two thousand sixteen

E Complete the sentences with your own information. Then share your sentences with a partner.

1. I was born in _____ . (year)

2. I traveled to _____ in _____ . (year)

3. I learned to _____ in _____ . (year)

4. I started to learn English in _____ . (year)

5. My family lived in _____ from _____ (year)
   to _____ (year).

LESSON TASK Talking about Your Life

A Think about important events in your life and write them in your notebook.

BRAINSTORMING

B Write your four most important events and years on the timeline.

ORGANIZING IDEAS

year

event

C Take turns telling your partner about your life events. Ask and answer follow-up questions using *wh-* words. Write your partner's events on this timeline.

A: *I graduated in 2009.*
B: *Where did you go to school?*
A: *I went to Waseda University in Tokyo.*

year

event

D Tell a larger group or your class about your partner. Give the dates and events. Add any details you discovered.

Video

Dinosaur Detective

MEET NIZAR IBRAHIM Nizar Ibrahim is a paleontologist. People call him "The Dinosaur Detective" because he hunts for dinosaur fossils and skeletons in the Sahara Desert.

Morocco
Algeria
Africa
Spinosaurus bones found

BEFORE VIEWING

A Look at the photos and map and read the captions. Answer the questions with a partner.

1. Who is Nizar Ibrahim? What is his job?
2. What do you think Ibrahim hunts for?
3. Where does Ibrahim work?

B Match each word from the video with its definition. Use your dictionary to help you.

1. _____ ecosystem
2. _____ fossil
3. _____ skeleton
4. _____ river
5. _____ extinct
6. _____ desert

a. something left from an ancient animal or plant

b. a large, hot, dry, sandy area

c. describes a plant or animal that lived on Earth in the past, but does not now

d. plants and animals in an area and how they exist together

e. the bones that create a human or animal form

f. a body of water such as the Nile or the Amazon

WHILE VIEWING

C ▶ 1.12 Watch the video and check (✓) all the adjectives Ibrahim uses to describe the Sahara Desert.

beautiful _____ cruel _____ full _____ mysterious _____ powerful _____
crazy _____ frightening _____ magical _____ peaceful _____ quiet _____

D ▶ 1.13 Watch the excerpt from the video. Number these events in the order that they happen.

_____ The tooth gets stuck in this little sand dune, in the river.

_____ A dinosaur loses a tooth.

__1__ A dinosaur is upstream.

_____ The tooth is carried downstream.

_____ The tooth is rolling on the riverbed.

AFTER VIEWING

E Discuss the questions with a partner.

CRITICAL THINKING: REFLECTING

1. In the video, Ibrahim says, "… in science, you sometimes have to be crazy." What does he mean by that? Do you agree with him?

2. Why is Ibrahim's work important?

A life-size model of a fossilized spinosaurus skeleton

B Vocabulary

A 🎧 2.27 Listen and check (✓) the words you already know. Then discuss their meaning with a partner. Check the dictionary for any you are not sure about.

☐ ancient (*adj*) ☐ culture (*n*) ☐ information (*n*) ☐ religion (*n*)
☐ century (*n*) ☐ history (*n*) ☐ peace (*n*) ☐ rules (*n*)

MEANING FROM
CONTEXT

B 🎧 2.28 Look at the photo and read the caption. Complete the conversation with the words in exercise A. Then listen and correct your answers.

A TRIP TO THE BRITISH MUSEUM

A: How was the British Museum?

B: It was amazing. You know that I love _____ and learning about the past.
$\quad$ 1

A: Where did you go in the museum?

B: Well, I started in the Asia Gallery. I really like Japanese _____ and
$\qquad\qquad\qquad\qquad\qquad$ 2
learning about their way of life.

A: What did you see there?

B: I saw _____ samurai armor* from the 16th _____ .
$\qquad$ 3 $\qquad\qquad$ 4

A: Oh, that's interesting! I want to see that. Did you take a picture? Or is that
against the _____ ?
$\qquad$ 5

B: No, it's allowed! Here's a Greek sculpture from the Parthenon in Athens!

A: That's a great picture! You know, I am interested in early _____ . Do
$\qquad\qquad\qquad$ 6
they have any Buddhist objects?

B: Yes, they do. You can get a map and more _____ at the desk
$\qquad\qquad\qquad$ 7
just inside the entrance.

A: Great. Thanks! I think I'll go next week. I need to take a break from school.

B: Good idea. You can always find _____ and quiet at the museum. It's
$\qquad$ 8
very relaxing.

---

*armor: metal clothing that protects soldiers or fighters

C Match each word from exercise A with its definition.

1. _____ ancient   a. people's way of living and customs

2. _____ century   b. things you can or cannot do

3. _____ information   c. the study of the past

4. _____ rules   d. a time of quiet and rest; no war

5. _____ culture   e. very old

6. _____ religion   f. facts about something

7. _____ peace   g. 100 years

8. _____ history   h. a system of beliefs about how to live

D Use a dictionary to find the adjective form/s for these words. Then share your words with the class.

Noun	Adjective
information	informative
religion	
history	
peace	
culture	

E Discuss the questions with a partner.

PERSONALIZING

1. What ancient treasures from your country do you know of? Describe them. Are they in a museum? Are any of them missing?

2. What is different or interesting about your culture? Name one thing.

◄ **Ancient Greek sculpture from the Parthenon in Athens, currently on display in the British Museum, London, UK**

Listening A Guided Tour of the British Museum

BEFORE LISTENING

PREVIEWING **A** In a small group, discuss the questions below.

1. What is in a history museum?
2. Where is the British Museum?
3. What do you think the photo on this page shows? What do you think the writing says?
4. Who makes the rules for a company? For a country? For a child at home? For a class?

WHILE LISTENING

LISTENING FOR
MAIN IDEAS **B** 🎧 2.29 Read the statements and answer choices. Then listen and choose the best answer to complete each statement.

1. Cyrus was a _____ ruler.
   a. strong
   b. dangerous
   c. lazy

2. The Cyrus Cylinder is important because there are _____ on it.
   a. rules, or laws, for living
   b. names of leaders
   c. dates of events

3. Cyrus _____ people of different religions.
   a. scared
   b. welcomed
   c. gave food to

▼ **The Cyrus Cylinder in the British Museum**

C 🎧 2.29 Listen again. Choose the best answer to complete each statement.

1. Cyrus started the first Persian Empire in the _____ century B.C.

   a. 5th
   b. 6th
   c. 7th

2. When was the Cyrus Cylinder written?

   a. 739 B.C.
   b. 1539
   c. 539 B.C.

3. On the cylinder, Cyrus tells his people they will _____ together.

   a. practice one religion
   b. live in peace
   c. fight wars

4. The Cyrus Cylinder was discovered in _____.

   a. 1867
   b. 1879
   c. 1897

NOTE-TAKING SKILL Using a Timeline

In lesson A, you used a timeline to help you present information. Timelines are also a good way to organize your notes as you listen. You can write dates and important information on the timeline to organize the events in history or in a story.

D 🎧 2.29 Listen again and complete the timeline with the important dates and information from the museum tour.

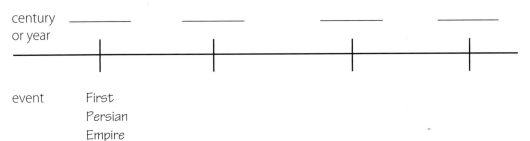

century
or year   _____   _____   _____   _____

event   First
             Persian
             Empire

AFTER LISTENING

E Discuss the questions with your group.

1. What can the leaders of our world learn from Cyrus?
2. What document does your country have that states the laws for the people?

B Speaking

CRITICAL THINKING:
REFLECTING

A Think of a treasure that you own. Using the sample answers as a guide, write your answers in the "You" column of the chart.

Questions	Sample Answers	You	Your Partner
1. What is a treasure you have?	A chessboard		
2. Where did you get it? / Who gave it to you?	From my father		
3. When did you get it? / What year did you get it?	In 2002, when I was 15		
4. Where do you keep it?	In my room		
5. How does it make you feel?	It makes me feel special and loved.		

B Work with a partner. Take turns asking and answering the questions in the chart. Take notes on your partner's answers in the last column of the chart.

A wooden chessboard for sale at the Pushkar Camel Fair, Pushkar, Rajasthan, India

C Form a group with another pair of students. Tell the group what you learned about your partner's "treasure." Ask questions to keep the conversation going.

A: *Mari has a chessboard. She got it from her father.*
B: *Oh really? Tell us more about that. What does it look like?*

FINAL TASK Presenting a Personal History

> You are going to give a presentation about yourself. You will create a timeline to show during your presentation. Visual aids such as a timeline can help make your presentation more interesting and understandable.

A Choose one of the topics. You will talk about a history of:

your English language learning   your country   your family   a friendship

B Create a timeline of the events for your topic. Add extra dates if you need to.   BRAINSTORMING

HISTORY OF MY _____

date

event

C Review the information in your timeline. Complete the sentences with the most interesting or important information.   ORGANIZING IDEAS

I want to tell you about _____

In _____ , _____

In _____ , _____

In _____ , _____

In _____ , _____

D Look at the sample presentation. Use it to practice your own presentation.

> **HISTORY OF MY FAMILY**
>
> *I want to tell you about the history of my family.*
>
> *My father's family is originally from Germany. In 1898, my great-grandparents moved to the United States from Germany. They moved to New York. Life was different, but they were happy. In 1934, my grandmother was born in New York. After my grandmother was born, my great-grandparents moved to Chicago. In 1950, my grandmother met my grandfather in high school. They got married in 1954. In 1959, my father was born. He met my mother in college, and they got married in 1985. Then, I was born in 1990. We all still live in Chicago.*

PRESENTATION SKILLS Body Language

Body language can help you communicate your ideas, and it can keep your audience interested. Body language can include:

- **Eye contact:** Look at different people in your audience; be sure to choose people on different sides of the room.
- **Facial expressions:** Smile or use other facial expressions to let your audience know how you feel.
- **Hand movements:** Describe sizes, shapes, or even feelings using your hands and arms.
- **Standing:** Stand tall and try to stay in one general area; do not walk around too much.

PRESENTING **E** Present your topic to your class. Make sure you point to your timeline during the presentation. Notice your body language. At the end of the presentation, ask the audience if there are any questions.

REFLECTION

1. What can you do to listen for reasons in a conversation or presentation?

_____

_____

2. Which do you think is more important: the search or the treasure?

_____

_____

3. Here are the vocabulary words from the unit. Check (✓) the ones you can use.

☐ ancient	☐ history	☐ peace
☐ century	☐ information	☐ religion
☐ culture **AWL**	☐ jewels	☐ rules
☐ find	☐ missing	☐ search
☐ gold	☐ mystery	
☐ hide	☐ object	

BREAKTHROUGHS

8

Close-up of a fingerprint in
a crime lab

THINK AND DISCUSS

1 What do you see in the photo? Where is it?
Why is it important?

2 A breakthrough is an important discovery.
Can you give an example of some kind of
breakthrough in the last 20 years?

141

EXPLORE THE THEME

Look at the images and read the information. Then discuss the questions.

1. What are cells? Who or what is made of cells?

2. What does the DNA in a cell do? How does it do that?

3. Why do scientists learn about cells and DNA? What do they do with the information? Give an example you know about.

DNA TODAY

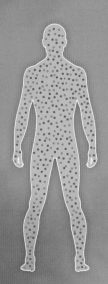

Center of a cell (the nucleus)

CELLS

A cell is the smallest part of all living things. Cells are too small to see. Humans are made of trillions of cells. This page is an image of the inside of a cell.

Each cell in a human has a job. Some help you see; others help you breathe, and so on. How do they know their job? Their "boss" tells them. Their boss is DNA.

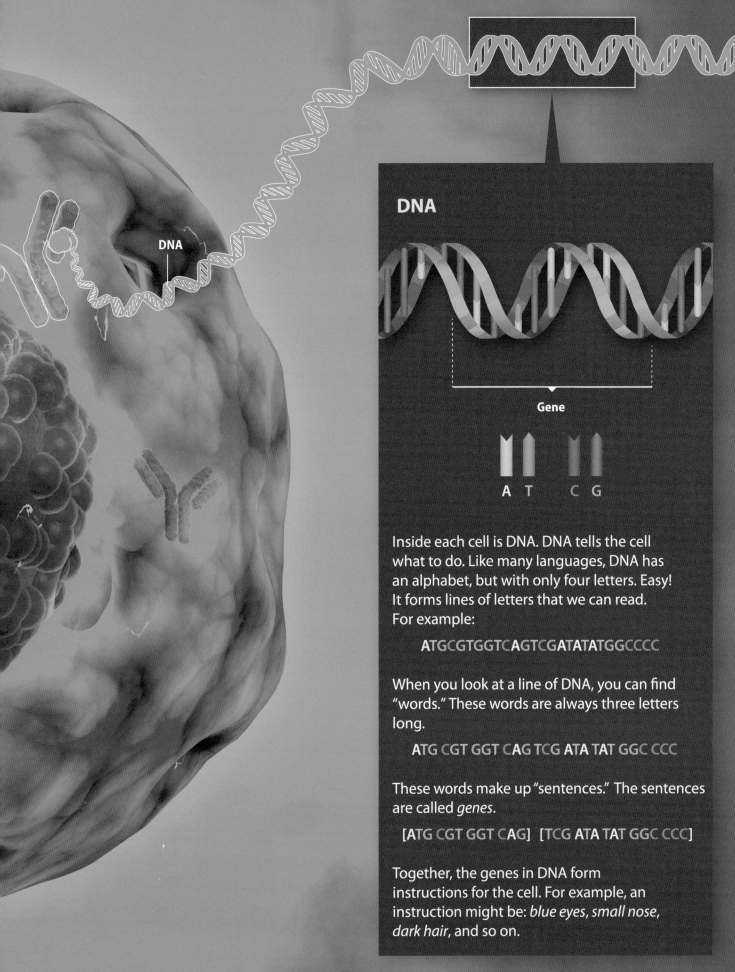

DNA

Gene

A T   C G

Inside each cell is DNA. DNA tells the cell what to do. Like many languages, DNA has an alphabet, but with only four letters. Easy! It forms lines of letters that we can read. For example:

ATGCGTGGTCAGTCGATATATGGCCCC

When you look at a line of DNA, you can find "words." These words are always three letters long.

ATG CGT GGT CAG TCG ATA TAT GGC CCC

These words make up "sentences." The sentences are called *genes*.

[ATG CGT GGT CAG] [TCG ATA TAT GGC CCC]

Together, the genes in DNA form instructions for the cell. For example, an instruction might be: *blue eyes*, *small nose*, *dark hair*, and so on.

A Vocabulary

A 🎧 2.30 Listen and check (✓) the words you already know. Then discuss their meaning with a partner. Check the dictionary for any you are not sure about.

☐ become (*v*)	☐ copy (*n*)	☐ expensive (*adj*)	☐ machine (*n*)
☐ control (*v*)	☐ exist (*v*)	☐ latest (*adj*)	☐ several (*adj*)

MEANING FROM
CONTEXT

B 🎧 2.31 Complete the sentences with the correct words from exercise A. Then listen and check your answers.

1. There are _____ ways DNA is used nowadays.

2. Each student has a _____ of the same test. There are no differences.

3. A robot is a type of _____ ; it is not a living thing.

4. I can _____ the robot by talking to it.

5. The toy robot dog is over $100; it's _____ .

6. He preferred teaching, so he didn't _____ an engineer.

7. Everyone wants the _____ smartphone because they think it's better than the last.

8. Smartphones didn't _____ before 2000.

C Write the correct word from exercise A next to its definition.

1. _____ a second version of the same thing

2. _____ a tool or object that uses power to do something

3. _____ to be present; to be alive

4. _____ to cause someone or something to do what you want

5. _____ to begin to be; start to have some quality

6. _____ some, but not many; more than a few

7. _____ costing a lot of money

8. _____ most recent; newest

▼ **Cloned longhorn calves in Austin, Texas, USA**

VOCABULARY SKILL Two-Part Verbs

Two-part verbs are verbs with two words and are very common, especially in speaking. The second word is usually a preposition or a particle (e.g., *to, in, on*). Common verbs, such as *come, get, take,* and *go,* often have different meanings in a two-part verb*. You can use a spider map to record new two-part verbs and their meanings.

from — to start or be from a place (*I **come from** Peru.*)

come — out — to be available to use or buy for the first time (*The new smartphone **came out** Friday.*)

over — to visit (*Can you **come over** to my house?*)

*These two-part verbs are sometimes called *phrasal verbs*.

D Read each definition and match it with the correct two-part verb. Then write an example sentence.

a. wake in the morning
b. return
c. to be friendly; have a good relationship
d. leave a bus or train

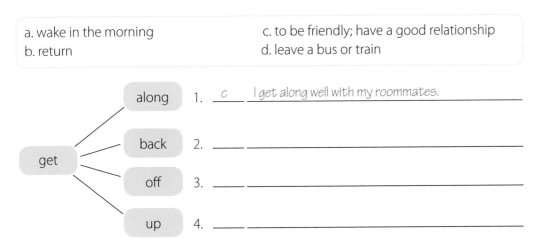

get — along   1. __c__ _I get along well with my roommates._

back   2. _____

off   3. _____

up   4. _____

E In your notebook, create a spider map for each of these common verbs: *go, break, bring, give,* and *take.* Use a dictionary to find at least two possible two-part verbs. Write their definitions and a sample sentence.

F Work with a partner. Complete the conversation with the correct preposition or particle of a two-part verb.

A: Hey, do you want to come _____ to study tonight? I didn't understand the lecture on cloning animals.
     ₁

B: Sure. I had some problems, too.

A: OK. Let's meet at my place at 6:00. I get _____ from class about then.
     ₂

B: Sounds good. I'm coming by bus. Do I get _____ at the Main Street bus stop?
     ₃

A: Are you are coming _____ campus?
     ₄

B: Yes.

A: Then get _____ at the Fifth Avenue stop.
     ₅

A Listening A Class Discussion about Cloning

BEFORE LISTENING

A Check (✓) the topics you know something about. Work in a small group. Share information about the topics.

_____ the movies *Jurassic Park* or *Jurassic World*

_____ cloning of animals such as farm animals or pets

_____ cloning of extinct animals such as dinosaurs

WHILE LISTENING

LISTENING FOR
MAIN IDEAS
B 🎧 2.32 Listen and check (✓) the two correct main ideas.

1. _____ The class is about cloning dinosaurs.

2. _____ The class is about cloning extinct animals.

3. _____ Cloning dinosaurs may be possible one day.

4. _____ Cloning animals may have good and bad points.

LISTENING FOR
DETAILS
C 🎧 2.32 Listen again and choose **T** for *True* or **F** for *False*.

1. *Jurassic Park* came out before *Jurassic World*.	T	F
2. *Jurassic Park* is a movie about dinosaur robots.	T	F
3. Clones are machines.	T	F
4. The first cloned animal lived six years.	T	F
5. Dolly was the only sheep ever cloned.	T	F
6. Scientists can clone some extinct animals.	T	F

▶ **The saber-toothed tiger is an extinct big cat that lived over 10,000 years ago.**

An opinion is someone's belief about something. Listening for opinions helps you understand a speaker's ideas. Listen for sentences starting with the following expressions:

> **In my opinion**, *dinosaurs are interesting.*
> **I think (that)** *dinosaurs are scary.*
> **I am not sure (that)** *cloning is a good idea.*
> **I don't like** *the idea of cloning. I* **prefer** *letting nature decide.*

D 🎧 **2.33** Listen to the excerpts and write the missing expressions. With a partner, discuss which opinions are *for* and which are *against* the idea of cloning. Write *F* for *for* or *A* for *against* next to each.

1. _____ it's a good idea at all.

2. _____ it's a good idea to clone them so they don't *become* extinct.

3. _____ it's a good idea to clone extinct animals.

4. _____ we should bring animals back.

AFTER LISTENING

NOTE-TAKING SKILL Using a T-Chart

When you are listening to a debate or other conversation where different opinions are expressed, you can take notes in a T-chart to help you organize the ideas. Put the positive opinions on the left in a "Pros" column and the negative opinions on the right in a "Cons" column.

Pros	Cons
ideas for	ideas against

E 🎧 **2.33** Listen to the excerpt from the conversation again. Write at least one reason *for* cloning and one more reason *against* it.

NOTE TAKING

Cloning Animals	
Pros (a good idea)	**Cons** (not a good idea)
	not natural; died for reason

F Compare your answers with a partner. Then discuss which opinion is most like yours.

A Speaking

A 🎧 2.34 Listen to the podcast about pet cloning. Write the modal you hear.

CLONING YOUR CAT: A GOOD IDEA?

In 2001, scientists at Texas A&M University cloned the first pet: CC the cat. Since then, cloning has become easier. This _____ mean big changes in
₁ the future.

Many pet lovers _____ start cloning their cats or dogs. Pet cloning
₂
companies _____ make a lot of money. There was one problem with
₃
CC the cat, though: she and her clone did not look the same. DNA does not always control a cat's color. CC had the same DNA, but the two cats were different colors.

People _____ want to risk getting a different-looking pet. Also, pet cloning
₄
costs from $50,000–$100,000. Most people _____ want to spend so much
₅
money. And, after all, they _____ just go to a shelter and get a pet for free.
₆

Finally, many other people _____ like the idea of cloning because
₇
animals _____ get hurt. What do you think?
₈

"CC" — the world's first cloned cat, produced at Texas A&M University in 2001

Kittens in a cage at a shelter for homeless animals

CRITICAL THINKING Considering Other Opinions

Many people have strong opinions about changes, especially in science and technology. Considering everyone's opinion, both for and against a topic, will help you form and support your own opinion.

B Work with a partner. For each opinion in the chart, think of an opposite opinion. Use the ideas in exercise A and your own ideas. Use modals of possibility to support your opinion.

Opinions For	Opinions Against
1. It's OK to clone a pet. It could help people.	_____ _____ _____
2. _____ _____ _____	I think it's too expensive to clone a pet. Someone could get a cat or dog at a shelter for free or not much money.
3. It would be very interesting to see real dinosaurs. It might teach us something about them.	_____ _____ _____
4. _____ _____ _____	Science-fiction movies are awful. I don't like them. I won't go to one. I prefer mysteries.

C Share your answers with your class. Remember to support your opinion using modals of possibility.

There are many ways to give an opinion. A speaker may:
* make a statement with an adjective.

  *That's so **scary**!*

  *That's a **great** idea.*

* use one of these common phrases to show an opinion.

  ***I think (that)** cloning animals might be useful.*

  ***In my opinion,** scientists need to be responsible.*

  ***I don't think (that)** newer is aways better.*

  ***I'm not sure** it is a good idea.*

D 🎧 **2.35** Listen to the conversation between Lara and Andy. Who expresses each opinion? Check (✓) the correct speaker.

Opinions	Lara	Andy
1. Cloning extinct animals is interesting.	☐	☐
2. Cloning extinct animals is not a good idea.	☐	☐
3. Cloning extinct animals is scary.	☐	☐
4. Cloning pets might be OK.	☐	☐
5. The science of cloning pets is amazing.	☐	☐
6. It's strange that cloned cats might look different.	☐	☐
7. Cloning pets is expensive.	☐	☐
8. It's better to get a cat that needs a home.	☐	☐

E 🎧 **2.35** Compare your answers in exercise D with a partner. Then listen again. Notice the words Lara and Andy use to express their opinions. Which phrase from the Speaking Skill box is used the most?

_____

EVERYDAY LANGUAGE Agreeing or Disagreeing with an Opinion

In a conversation or discussion, you will often agree or disagree with someone's opinion. Here are common expressions you can use.

Agree	**Disagree**
I agree.	*I'm not sure I agree.*
Absolutely!	*I don't think so.*
Good point.	*I disagree.*

F For each opinion in exercise D, tell your partner your own opinion. Use a phrase from the Speaking Skill box and agree or disagree using phrases from the Everyday Language box.

A: ***In my opinion,** cloning is a bad idea. **I think** it could cause problems.*

B: *Really? **I disagree. I think** it might help protect animals.*

LESSON TASK Group Debates on Cloning

A Follow these steps to complete the survey.

1. Work in a group of three. Read the survey opinions. Discuss a final opinion to add to the survey. Write the opinion in row 5.

2. Write *A* if you agree, *D* if you disagree, and *NS* if you are not sure in the column *My Opinions*.

3. Take turns sharing your opinions with your two group members. Write their answers in the last two columns.

CLONING: CLASS SURVEY	MY OPINIONS	CLASSMATE 1	CLASSMATE 2
1. I think it's OK to clone any extinct animal.			
2. I believe it's OK to clone some extinct animals or endangered animals, but not all.			
3. I think cloning cats and dogs for people is OK.			
4. I think cloning a person one day is a good idea.			
5. Your idea _____			

B As a group, discuss your results. Which opinions did you agree on? Which did you feel differently about?

> *Rosa and Soon Yi don't think it's a good idea to clone extinct animals, but I think sometimes it's OK.*

C Follow these steps to debate opinions about cloning.

1. Your teacher will give each group an opinion from exercise A to defend (even if you don't agree with it!).
2. Your group will be paired with another group who has the opposite opinion.
3. You will debate the other group for 5 minutes.
4. The rest of the class listens and decides which group had a stronger argument.
5. Repeat with the other groups.

Video

Dr. Helena Ndume with a happy patient

A Chance to See Again

DR. HELENA NDUME is an eye doctor from Namibia. She grew up as a refugee and worked hard to become an eye doctor. She then returned to Namibia to help the blind. She has helped over 35,000 patients. Dr. Ndume was the first person to receive the United Nations Nelson Mandela Prize.

BEFORE VIEWING

A Match each word from the video with its definition. Use your dictionary to help you.

1. _____ blind (*adj*)
2. _____ fortunate (*adj*)
3. _____ give back (*phr. v*)
4. _____ patients (*n*)
5. _____ screening (*n*)
6. _____ transformed (*v*)

a. to help people who have less than you
b. people who go to the doctor
c. changed
d. lucky
e. tests to help a doctor understand a patient
f. unable to see

CRITICAL THINKING:
ANALYZING VISUALS

B Look at the map. Then discuss the questions with a partner.

1. Where is the problem of blindness the worst? Where is it less serious?
2. Why do you think the problem is worse in some places than others?

WHILE VIEWING

C ▶ 1.14 Watch the video. Discuss the questions with a partner.

UNDERSTANDING MAIN IDEAS

1. The radio announcer tells people about an *eye camp*. What do you think an *eye camp* is?

2. How did some people feel about the eye camp at first?

3. Why do you think they changed their minds the second year?

D ▶ 1.14 Watch the video again. Complete each statement with a word from the box.

UNDERSTANDING DETAILS

82	help	hurt
family	hospital	thousands

1. The eye camp is at a _____ .

2. The radio speaker says to bring your _____ .

3. _____ people came to the first eye camp.

4. Many people believed Dr. Ndume might _____ their eyes.

5. The next year, _____ of people came to the eye camp.

6. Dr. Ndume believes you should _____ people who have less than you.

AFTER VIEWING

E Work in a group. What are ways people "give back" or help people in your city or hometown? Share your answers with your group.

PERSONALIZING

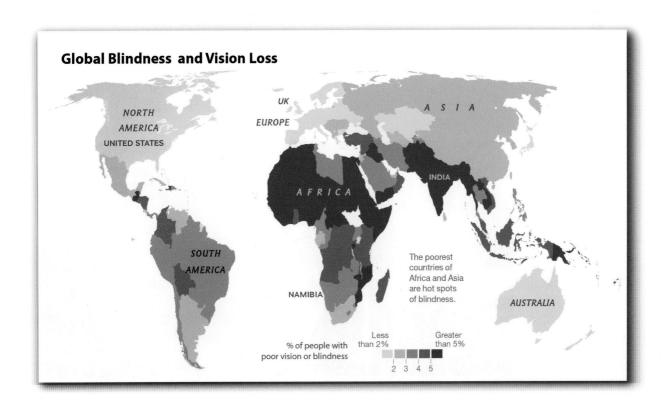

Global Blindness and Vision Loss

UK
EUROPE
NORTH AMERICA
UNITED STATES
ASIA
INDIA
AFRICA
SOUTH AMERICA
NAMIBIA
AUSTRALIA

The poorest countries of Africa and Asia are hot spots of blindness.

% of people with poor vision or blindness

Less than 2%   Greater than 5%

2 3 4 5

B Vocabulary

A 🎧 2.36 Listen and check (✓) the words you already know.

☐ bone (*n*) ☐ healthy (*adj*) ☐ parts (*n*) ☐ simple (*adj*)

☐ consider (*v*) ☐ heart (*n*) ☐ replace (*v*) ☐ treatment (*n*)

MEANING FROM CONTEXT

B 🎧 2.37 Read and listen to *Science News Now*. Notice each word in blue and think about its meaning.

SCIENCE NEWS NOW

3-D Body Parts!

Scientists say they can now print live body **parts** on 3-D printers. If you need a new arm or leg **bone**, for example, doctors might soon be able to **replace** yours with one from a 3-D printer. They may also be able to print an organ such as a stomach or a **heart**. For more information, ...

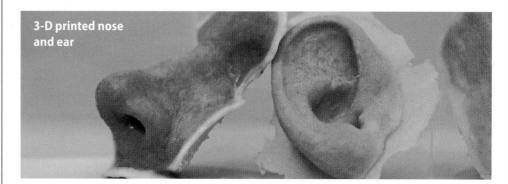

3-D printed nose and ear

New Treatment to Help You See!

Do you know someone who is blind or has poor vision? A new **treatment** is now available. It is helping many people to see again. **Consider** the changes it could bring to their lives. For more information, ...

Woman having an eye exam

Cheap DNA Tests!
Are you going to be healthy in the future? Find out with cheap DNA tests. Learn about your DNA for just $100! Several companies will do a **simple** test for you. Soon after, they will send you the results. With this information, you can learn about your genes. You can see if you are **healthy**. You can also research your family and find cousins you didn't know about. For more information,…

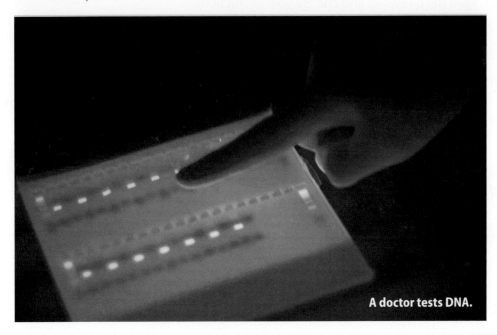

A doctor tests DNA.

C Write the correct word from exercise A to complete each sentence.

1. When I was skiing last year, I broke a _____ in my leg. It's fine now.

2. Please _____ the job. We think you are perfect for it.

3. I passed the biology test. A few questions were hard, but most were very
   _____ .

4. Aspirin is a common _____ for headaches and other pain.

5. Usually Javier is very _____ , but this week he's sick.

6. I need to buy a few _____ before I fix the car.

7. I just ran five miles! My _____ is beating very fast.

8. The refrigerator in the lab is old. We need to _____ it.

D With your partner, take turns asking and answering these questions.   PERSONALIZING

1. Have you ever broken a bone? Which one? How did you do it?

2. Read the stories in exercise B again. Which do you want to know more about? Which might you research more online? Explain.

3. Do you eat well and exercise? Could you be healthier? How? List two or three simple ways.

Listening A Lecture on Ending Blindness

BEFORE LISTENING

PREDICTING **A** Read the questions and choose your predictions.

1. About how many blind people are there in the world?

   a. 1 out of 20   b. 1 out of 200   c. 1 out of 2,000

2. Which countries have more blindness?

   a. low income   b. high income

3. Is all blindness easy to fix now?

   a. yes   b. no

WHILE LISTENING

LISTENING FOR MAIN IDEAS

B 🎧 2.38 ▶ 1.15 Listen to the first part of the lecture. Choose the correct answers.

PART 1

1. With a simple treatment, _____ of all blind people could see now.

   a. 20 percent   b. 50 percent

2. Scientists believe that _____ new treatments will help to end all other causes of blindness.

   a. two   b. three

3. The problem of blindness is bigger among _____ people.

   a. poor   b. rich

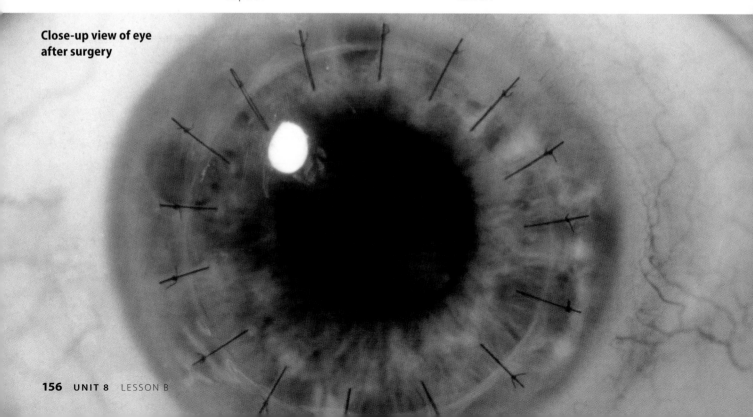

Close-up view of eye after surgery

C 🎧 2.39 ▶ 1.16 Listen to the second part of the lecture. Then complete the main ideas in Part 2 with possible correct words. More than one answer may be possible.

LISTENING FOR MAIN IDEAS

PART 2

Treatment	Main Idea
1. Cell therapy	Doctors replace _____ eye cells with _____ eye cells.
2. Stem cells	Doctors put stem cells in the _____ . They _____ and become the missing part.
3. Bionic eye parts	Doctors _____ part of the eye with a man-made eye _____ .

D 🎧 2.40 Listen to the whole lecture. Choose the correct answers.

LISTENING FOR DETAILS

1. (39 / 59) million people in the world are blind.

2. Only (10 / 20) percent of blind people are from high-income countries.

3. Researchers believe an end to blindness is (20 / 50) years away.

4. The (smallest / most important) part of a plant, animal, or person is a cell.

5. You get your DNA and genes from (growing up / your parents). They make you *you*.

6. A bionic body part is (natural / a machine).

7. A (stem / DNA) cell is a basic cell before it becomes another type of cell, such as a skin or bone cell.

8. The three treatments (already / don't yet) work all the time.

E Look back at your predictions in exercise A. Which ones were correct? Tell a partner.

CHECKING PREDICTIONS

AFTER LISTENING

F Work in a group. What are some pros and cons of using DNA research to treat people? Complete the chart with your ideas.

CRITICAL THINKING: EVALUATING

DNA Research in Medicine	
Pros (a good idea)	**Cons** (not a good idea)

Speaking

PRONUNCIATION Schwa /ə/ in Unstressed Syllables

🎧 2.41 In words and sentences, there are stressed and unstressed syllables. The vowels in unstressed syllables are often not fully pronounced. The vowels often sound like schwa /ə/. Listen to these examples. The vowels in the underlined syllables sound like schwa.

*be**come***   *ma**chine***   *re**place***

The modals *can* and *could* are usually unstressed in a sentence. Their vowels often sound like schwa.

*The patient can **see** now.*
*The company could **earn** over one million dollars this year.*

A 🎧 2.42 Listen and repeat the words. Underline the syllable(s) with the schwa sound.

1. bi-o-<u>lo</u>-gy
2. tech-no-lo-gy
3. ther-a-py
4. pro-blem
5. com-pu-ter
6. sci-en-tist
7. con-trol
8. cri-mi-nal

B 🎧 2.43 Listen and complete the paragraph. Then take turns reading it with a partner. Respond to the question at the end by sharing your ideas with your partner.

NEW BREAKTHROUGH IN FIGHTING CRIME

_____ are using DNA from crime scenes in a new way. They are _____ better at understanding the meaning of genes every year. By looking at the DNA, they _____ tell us hair color, face shape, and other _____ about a person's body. In many _____ stations around the United States, _____ programmers can create a face that may look like the person who did the crime. This is amazing _____ , but _____ it be dangerous? What do you think?

Police use a technology called *DNA phenotyping* to create the face of a possible criminal.

Researcher testing a blood sample

C How else is DNA research used? Look at the following jobs where people use DNA research. Check (✓) any you know something about. Add another idea to the list if you can. Discuss your ideas with a partner.

> *Biologists look at the DNA of plants to learn about them and discover relationships between them.*

_____ biologists/earth scientists   _____ lawyers

_____ historians/archaeologists   _____ computer scientists

_____ police   Your idea: _____

FINAL TASK Group Presentation: DNA in the Real World

You will give a group presentation about one way DNA science is used in real life (e.g., cloning, health/doctors, police, and so on). You can use information from the unit, from your own knowledge, or from research online or anywhere else.

A With a group of three, decide on one area of DNA research that interests you. Use the ideas in the unit or your own ideas.

_____

B Discuss any information you already know with your group. Take notes.   BRAINSTORMING

_____

_____

_____

C Use this outline to plan your group presentation. Take notes below or in your notebook.

I Introduction to area of research (What is it? Who uses it? How do they use it?)

_____

_____

II Positive impact (What is a good use of it? How does it help?)

_____

III Negative impacts/other opinions (Could it hurt people, animals, or the environment? How might some people feel about it? Why do you think it is OK or not OK?)

_____

_____

PRESENTATION SKILL Using Questions

Presenters often use questions to prepare their listeners to hear important information. First, ask the question and wait a moment to allow your listeners to think about possible answers. Then answer the question. Giving your audience time to think will help them better understand and remember the important points.

> _Today's lecture is about blindness, or, rather, a future without blindness._ **How can we help people who cannot see?** ... _Well, 50 percent of these people ..._

D Think of two possible questions you could ask during your presentation. Write them here. Decide when to ask them. Insert them where you think is best.

_____

_____

E With your group, present your area of interest to the class. Each person in your group should present one part of the presentation.

REFLECTION

1. Why is it important to consider other opinions? Give examples and explain your ideas.

_____

_____

2. After reading the unit, are you happy about the changes science is making in our lives? Give reasons.

_____

_____

3. Here are the vocabulary words from the unit. Check (✔) the ones you can use.

☐ become   ☐ expensive   ☐ replace

☐ bone   ☐ healthy   ☐ several

☐ control   ☐ heart   ☐ simple

☐ consider   ☐ latest   ☐ treatment

☐ copy   ☐ machine

☐ exist   ☐ part

Independent Student Handbook

LISTENING SKILLS

Predicting

Speakers giving formal talks usually begin by introducing themselves and their topic. Listen carefully to the introduction of the topic so that you can predict what the talk will be about.

Strategies:

- Use visual information including titles on the board or on presentation slides.
- Think about what you already know about the topic.
- Ask yourself questions that you think the speaker might answer.
- Listen for specific phrases that indicate an introduction (e.g., *My topic is…*).

Listening for Main Ideas

It's important to be able to tell the difference between a speaker's main ideas and supporting details. It is more common for teachers to test students' understanding of main ideas than of specific details.

Strategies:

- Listen carefully to the introduction. Speakers often state the main idea in the introduction.
- Listen for rhetorical questions, or questions that the speaker asks, and then answers. Often the answer is the statement of the main idea.
- Notice words and phrases that the speaker repeats. Repetition often signals main ideas.

Listening for Details (Examples)

A speaker often provides examples that support a main idea. A good example can help you understand and remember the main idea better.

Strategies:

- Listen for specific phrases that introduce examples.
- Listen for general statements. Examples often follow general statements.

Listening for Details (Reasons)

Speakers often give reasons or list causes and/or effects to support their ideas.

Strategies:

- Notice nouns that might signal causes/reasons (e.g., *factors, influences, causes, reasons*) or effects/results (e.g., *effects, results, outcomes, consequences*).
- Notice verbs that might signal causes/reasons (e.g., *contribute to, affect, influence, determine, produce*) or effects/results (e.g., *is affected by, result in*).

Understanding Meaning from Context

When you are not familiar with a word that a speaker says, you can sometimes guess the meaning of the word using the context or situation.

Strategies:

- Don't panic. You don't always understand every word in your first language, either.
- Use context clues to understand the general idea. What did you understand just before or just after the missing part? What did the speaker probably say?
- Listen for words and phrases that signal a definition or explanation (e.g., *What that means is…*).

Recognizing a Speaker's Bias

Speakers often have an opinion about the topic they are discussing. It's important for you to know if they are presenting all the facts, or only the facts that support their opinion. The speaker may use certain language when they have a strong bias.

Strategies:

- Notice words like adjectives, adverbs, and modals that the speaker uses (e.g., *ideal, horribly, should, shouldn't*). These suggest that the speaker has a bias.
- Listen to the speaker's voice. Does he or she sound excited, angry, or bored?
- Notice if the speaker gives more weight or attention to one point of view over another.
- Listen for words that signal opinions (e.g., *I think…*).

NOTE-TAKING SKILLS

Taking notes is a personalized skill. It is important to develop a note-taking system that works for you. However, there are some common strategies to improve your note taking.

Before You Listen

Focus

Try to clear your mind before the speaker begins so you can pay attention. If possible, review previous notes or think about what you already know about the topic.

Predict

If you know the topic of the talk, think about what you might hear.

Listen

Take Notes by Hand

Research suggests that taking notes by hand rather than on a computer is more effective. Taking notes by hand requires you to summarize, rephrase, and synthesize information. This helps you *encode* the information, or put it into a form that you can understand and remember.

Listen for Signal Words and Phrases

Speakers often use signal words and phrases (e.g., *Today we're going to talk about…*) to organize their ideas and show relationships between them. Listening for signal words and phrases can help you decide what information to write in your notes.

Condense (Shorten) Information

- As you listen, focus on the most important ideas. The speaker will usually repeat, define, explain, and/or give examples of these ideas. Take notes on these ideas.

  Speaker: *The Itaipú Dam provides about 20% of the electricity used in Brazil, and about 75% of the electricity used in Paraguay. That electricity goes to millions of homes and businesses, so it's good for the economy of both countries.*

  Notes: Itaipú Dam → electricity: Brazil 20%, Paraguay 75%

- Don't write full sentences. Write only key words (nouns, verbs, adjectives, and adverbs), phrases, or short sentences.

  Full sentence: *Teachers are normally at the top of the list of happiest jobs.*

  Notes: teachers happiest

- Leave out information that is obvious.

  Full sentence: *Photographer Annie Griffiths is famous for her beautiful photographs. She travels all over the world to take photos.*

  Notes: Photographer A. Griffiths travels world

- Write numbers and statistics. (9 bil; 35%)
- Use abbreviations (e.g., *ft., min., yr*) and symbols (=, ≠, >, <, %, →)
- Use indenting. Write main ideas on left side of paper. Indent details.
  Benefits of eating ugly foods
  Save $
  10-20% on ugly fruits & vegs. at market
- Write details under key terms to help you remember them.
- Write the definitions of important new words.

After You Listen

- Review your notes soon after the lecture or presentation. Add any details you missed.
- Clarify anything you don't understand in your notes with a classmate or teacher.
- Add or highlight main ideas. Cross out details that aren't important or necessary.
- Rewrite anything that is hard to read or understand. Rewrite your notes in an outline or other graphic organizer to organize the information more clearly.
- Use arrows, boxes, diagrams, or other visual cues to show relationships between ideas.

ORGANIZING INFORMATION

Use graphic organizers to take notes, or to organize your notes.

Spider maps show relationships.

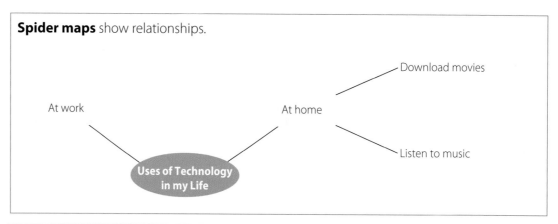

T-charts compare two topics.

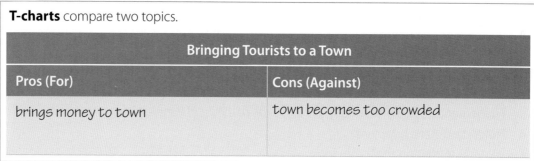

Bringing Tourists to a Town	
Pros (For)	**Cons (Against)**
brings money to town	town becomes too crowded

Timelines show a sequence of events.

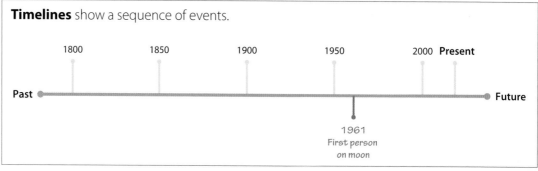

Venn diagrams show the differences and similarities between two or more things.

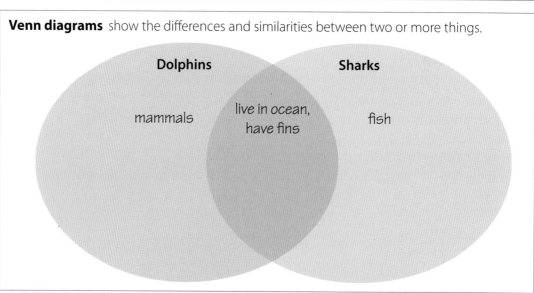

SPEAKING: PHRASES FOR CLASSROOM COMMUNICATION

Phrases for Expressing Yourself

Expressing Opinions
I think…	*In my opinion/view…*
I believe…	*Personally,…*
I'm (not) sure…	*To me,…*

Expressing Likes and Dislikes
I like…	*I hate…*
I prefer…	*I really don't like…*
I love…	*I don't care for…*

Giving Facts
Studies show…

Researchers found…

The record shows…

Giving Tips or Suggestions
You/We should/shouldn't/could…

You/We ought to…

It's (not) a good idea to…

Let's…

Why don't we/you…

Agreeing
I agree.	*Absolutely.*
True.	*Definitely.*
Good point.	*Right!*
Exactly.	

Disagreeing
I disagree.

I'm not so sure about that.

I don't know.

That's a good point, but I don't agree.

Useful Phrases for Classroom Discussions

Checking Your Understanding
So are you saying that…?

So what you mean is…?

What do you mean?

Do you mean…?

I'm not sure what you mean.

Asking for Repetition
Could you say that again?

I'm sorry?

I didn't catch what you said.

I'm sorry. I missed that. What did you say?

Could you repeat that please?

Checking Others' Understanding
Does that make sense?

Do you understand?

Is that clear?

Do you have any questions?

Asking for Opinions
What do you think?

Do you have any thoughts?

What are your thoughts?

What's your opinion?

Taking Turns
Can/May I say something?

Could I add something?

Your turn.

You go ahead.

Interrupting Politely
Excuse me.

Pardon me.

Forgive me for interrupting, but…

I hate to interrupt, but…

Making Small Talk
What do you do? (job)

Can you believe this weather?

How about this weather?

What do you do in your free time?

What do you do for fun?

Showing Interest
I see.	*Good for you.*
Really?	*Seriously?*
Um-hmm.	*No kidding!*
Wow.	*And? (Then what?)*
That's funny / amazing / incredible / awful!	

PRESENTATION STRATEGIES

You will often have to give individual or group presentations in your class. The strategies below will help you to prepare, present, and reflect on your presentations.

Prepare

Consider Your Topic

- **Choose a topic you feel passionate about.** If you are passionate about your topic, your audience will be more interested and excited about your topic, too.

Consider Your Purpose

- **Have a strong start.** Use a quote, an interesting example, a rhetorical question, or a powerful image to get your audience's attention. Include one sentence that explains what you will do in your presentation and why.
- **Stay focused.** Make sure your details and examples support your main points. Avoid unnecessary information that takes you away from your topic.
- **Use visuals that relate to your ideas.** Drawings, photos, video clips, infographics, charts, maps, slides, and physical objects can get your audience's attention and explain ideas effectively. For example, a photo or map of a location you mention can help your audience picture a place they have never been. Visuals should be bright, clear, and simple.
- **Have a strong conclusion.** A strong conclusion is as important as a strong start. Good conclusions often refer back to the introduction, or beginning of the presentation. For example, if you ask a question in the beginning, you can answer it in the conclusion. Remember to restate your main points.

Consider your Audience

- **Use familiar ideas.** Think about the people in your audience. Ask yourself these questions: Where are they from? How old are they? What is their background? What do they already know about my topic? What information do I need to explain? Use language and ideas they will understand.
- **Share a personal story.** Consider presenting information that will get an emotional reaction; for example, information that will make your audience feel surprised, curious, worried, or upset. This will help your audience relate to you and your topic.
- **Be authentic (be yourself!).** Write your presentation yourself. Use words that you know and are comfortable using.

Rehearse

- **Make an outline** to help you organize your ideas.
- **Write notes on notecards.** Do not write full sentences, just key words and phrases to help you remember important ideas. Mark the words you should stress and places to pause.
- **Review pronunciation.** Check the pronunciation of words you are uncertain about. Note and practice the pronunciation of difficult words.
- **Memorize the introduction and conclusion.** Practice your presentation several times. Practice saying it out loud to yourself (perhaps in front of a mirror or video recorder) and in front of others.
- **Ask for feedback.** If something isn't clear or doesn't work, change it.

Present

- **Pay attention to your pacing** (how fast or slow you speak). Remember to speak slowly and clearly. Pause to allow your audience time to process the information.
- **Speak loud enough to be heard** by everyone in the audience, but not too loud. Ask the audience if your volume is OK at the beginning of your talk.
- **Vary your intonation.** Don't speak in the same tone throughout the talk. Your audience will be more interested if your voice rises and falls, speeds up and slows down to match the ideas you are talking about.
- **Be friendly and relaxed with your audience**—remember to smile!
- **Show enthusiasm for your topic.** Use humor if appropriate.
- **Have a relaxed body posture.** Don't stand with your arms folded, or look down at your notes. Use body language when helpful to emphasize your points.
- **Don't read directly from your notes.** Use them to help you remember ideas.
- **Don't look at or read from your visuals too much.** Use them to support your ideas.
- **Make frequent eye contact** with the entire audience.

Reflect

- **Consider what you think went well** during your presentation and what areas you can improve upon.
- **Get feedback** from your classmates and teacher. How do their comments relate to your own thoughts about your presentation? Did they notice things you didn't? How can you use their feedback in your next presentation?

PRESENTATION OUTLINE

When you are planning a presentation, you may find it helpful to use an outline. If it is a group presentation, the outline can provide an easy way to divide the content. For example, one student can do the introduction, another student the first idea in the body, and so on.

1. Introduction

Topic: _____

Hook: _____

Statement of main idea: _____

2. Body

First step/example/reason: _____

    Supporting details: _____   _____   _____

Second step/example/reason: _____

    Supporting details: _____   _____   _____

Third step/example/reason: _____

    Supporting details: _____   _____   _____

3. Conclusion

Main points to summarize: _____   _____

Suggestions/Predictions: _____

Closing comments/summary: _____

_____

PRONUNCIATION GUIDE

Sounds and Symbols

Vowels

Symbol	Key Words
/ɑ/	hot, stop
/æ/	cat, ran
/aɪ/	fine, nice
/i/	eat, need
/ɪ/	sit, him
/eɪ/	name, say
/ɛ/	get, bed
/ʌ/	cup, what
/ə/	about, lesson
/u/	boot, new
/ʊ/	book, could
/oʊ/	go, road
/ɔ/	law, walk
/aʊ/	house, now
/ɔɪ/	toy, coin

Consonants

Symbol	Key Words	Symbol	Key Words
/b/	boy	/t/	tea
/d/	day	/tʃ/	cheap, watch
/dʒ/	job, bridge	/v/	vote, have
/f/	face	/w/	we
/g/	go	/y/	yes
/h/	hat	/z/	zoo, is
/k/	key, car		
/l/	love	/ð/	they, father
/m/	my	/θ/	think, both
/n/	nine	/ʃ/	shoe, wash
/ŋ/	sing	/ʒ/	measure
/p/	pen		
/r/	right		
/s/	see		

Source: *The Newbury House Dictionary plus Grammar Reference,* Fifth Edition, National Geographic Learning/ Cengage Learning, 2014.

Rhythm

Stress

• English words are based on syllables—units of sound that include one vowel sound.

• In every word in English, one syllable has the primary stress. It is louder and clearer than the other syllables.

• In sentences, new ideas and information are usually stressed.

Pausing

• Pauses in English can be divided into two groups: long and short pauses.

• Long pauses are used to mark the end of a thought.

• Short pauses are used to break up the ideas in sentences into smaller, easier to understand chunks of information.

Intonation

English speakers use intonation (the rise and fall of their voice) to help express meaning. For example, speakers usually use a rising intonation at the end of *yes/no* questions, and a falling intonation at the end of statments and *wh-* questions.

VOCABULARY BUILDING STRATEGIES

Guessing Meaning from Context

You can often guess the meaning of an unfamiliar word by looking at or listening to the words and sentences around it. Speakers usually know when a word is new to the audience or is important for understanding the main ideas, and they often provide clues to its meaning.

■ Repetition: A speaker may use the same key word, or use another form of the same word.

■ Restatement or synonym: A speaker may give a synonym to explain the meaning of a word, using phrases such as, *in other words, also called, or,* and *also known as.*

■ Antonyms: A speaker may define a word by explaining what it is NOT. The speaker may say *Unlike A, B is…* or *In contrast to A, B is…*

■ Definition: Listen for signals such as *which means* or *is defined as.* Definitions can also be signaled by a pause.

■ Examples: A speaker may provide examples that can help you figure out what something is. For example, **Mascots** *are a very popular marketing tool. You've seen them on commercials and in ads on social media –* **cute, brightly colored creatures that help sell a product**.

Understanding Word Families: Roots, Prefixes, and Suffixes

Use your understanding of roots, prefixes, and suffixes to recognize unfamiliar words and to expand your vocabulary. The root part of the word (also called the *stem*) provides the main meaning. A prefix comes before the root and usually changes the meaning (e.g., adding *re-* to a word means "again" or "back"). A suffix comes after the root and usually changes the part of speech (e.g., adding *-tion* to a verb changes it to a noun). Words that share the same root belong to the same word family (e.g., *event, eventful, uneventful*).

Prefix	Meaning	Example
dis-	not, opposite of	disappear, dislike
un-, im-	not	unfinished, impossible
inter-	between	Internet, international
mis-	badly, incorrectly	misunderstand, misuse
pre-	before	preheat, prepare
re-	again; back	repeat; return
trans-	across, beyond	transfer, translate

Suffix	Meaning	Example
-able, -ible	worth, ability	believable, impossible
-ful	full of	beautiful, successful
-ion, -tion, -ation	the action of	occasion, education, foundation
-ize	to make	realize, privatize
-ly	in the manner of	quickly, happily
-ment	result of an action	excitement, treatment

Tips for Using a Dictionary

- When you see or hear a new word, try to guess its part of speech (noun, verb, adjective, etc.) and meaning before you look it up in a dictionary.
- Some words have many meanings. Look up a new word in the dictionary and try to choose the correct meaning for the context.
- When you look up a word, look at all the definitions to see if there is a basic meaning. This will help you understand the word when it is used in a different context. Also look at all the related words, or words in the same family. This can help you expand your vocabulary. For example, the core meaning of *structure* is *something built or put together*.

> **structure** / ˈstrʌktʃər/ *n.* **1** [C] a building of any kind: *A new structure is being built on the corner.* **2** [C] any architectural object of any kind: *The Eiffel Tower is a famous Parisian structure.* **3** [U] the way parts are put together or organized: *the structure of a song‖a business's structure*
> –*v.* [T] **-tured, -turing, -tures** to put together or organize parts of s.t.: *We are structuring a plan to hire new teachers.*
> –*adj.* **structural.**

Source: *The Newbury House Dictionary plus Grammar Reference*, Fifth Edition, National Geographic Learning/Cengage Learning, 2014

Multi-Word Units

You can improve your fluency if you learn and use vocabulary as multi-word units (sometimes called *chunks*). Some multi-word units include idioms (*up in the air*), collocations (*interested in*), and fixed expressions (*in other words*). Keep track of multi-word units in a notebook or on notecards.

Vocabulary Note Cards

You can expand your vocabulary by using vocabulary note cards. Write the word, expression, or sentence that you want to learn on one side. On the other, draw a four-square grid and write the following in the squares: the definition, the translation (in your first language), a sample sentence, and any synonyms.

definition:	first language translation:
sample sentence:	synonyms:

Use the cards every day to test yourself or a partner.

VOCABULARY INDEX

Word	Page	CEFR† Level	Word	Page	CEFR Level
according to	104	B1	die	84	A1
adult*	14	A1	difficult	84	A1
adventure	84	A2	discover	94	B1
advice	34	A2	download	64	A2
amazing	54	A2	effect	74	B1
ancient	134	B1	enjoy	34	A1
area*	44	A2	equipment*	64	B1
available*	74	A2	especially	104	A2
beautiful	44	A1	exciting	24	A1
become	144	A2	exist	144	B1
behavior /			expensive	144	A1
behaviour	114	B1	experience	64	B1
believe	104	A2	fail	34	A2
benefit*	64	B1	famous	44	A1
body	84	A1	favorite /		
bone	154	B1	favourite	4	A1
boring	24	A1	find	124	A1
boss	24	A1	forest	94	A2
brain	74	A2	friendly	4	A2
century	134	A2	garden	114	A1
change	14	A1	goal*	94	A2
climb	84	A2	gold	124	A2
company	34	A2	grow up	14	A2
consider	154	B1	guest	114	A2
contact*	34	A2	habit	104	B1
control	144	B1	hard	64	A1
copy	144	A2	health	74	A2
count	94	B1	healthy	154	A2
create*	24	B1	heart	154	A2
criminal	114	B1	hide	124	B1
crowded	44	A2	history	134	A2
culture*	134	B1	hobby	4	A2
danger	94	A2	hurt	74	A2
decrease	94	B1	increase	114	B1
depend on	74	B1	information	134	A2

†The Common European Framework of Reference for Languages (CEFR) is an international standard for describing language proficiency. *Pathways Foundations* is intended for students at CEFR levels A1–A2. The target vocabulary is at the following CEFR levels: A1: 20%; A2: 43%; B1: 33%; B2: 2%; C1: 0%; C2: 0%; off list: 1%.

*These words are on the Academic Word List (AWL). The AWL is a list of the 570 highest-frequency academic word families that regularly appear in academic texts. The AWL was compiled by researcher Averil Coxhead based on her analysis of a 3.5-million-word corpus (Coxhead, 2000).

RUBRICS

UNIT 1 FINAL TASK Giving a Presentation about Yourself

Check (✓) if the presenter:	Presenter or Group		
	_____	_____	_____
1. answered the question "What is important in your life?"	☐	☐	☐
2. used correct forms and pronunciation of *be*	☐	☐	☐
3. used a pie chart	☐	☐	☐
4. made eye contact with the audience	☐	☐	☐
OVERALL RATING Note: 1 = lowest; 5 = highest	1 2 3 4 5	1 2 3 4 5	1 2 3 4 5
NOTES:			

UNIT 2 FINAL TASK Presenting your Dream Job

Check (✓) if the presenter:	Presenter or Group		
	_____	_____	_____
1. spoke clearly about a dream job	☐	☐	☐
2. used correct forms and pronunciation of simple present	☐	☐	☐
3. used listing words	☐	☐	☐
4. used phrases to close the presentation	☐	☐	☐
OVERALL RATING Note: 1 = lowest; 5 = highest	1 2 3 4 5	1 2 3 4 5	1 2 3 4 5
NOTES:			

UNIT 3   FINAL TASK Presenting Class Survey Results

Check (✓) if the presenter:	Presenter or Group		
	_____	_____	_____
1. spoke clearly about classmates	☐	☐	☐
2. stated the survey question and gave the results	☐	☐	☐
3. used a correct and clear bar graph	☐	☐	☐
4. used useful phrases to present a bar graph	☐	☐	☐
OVERALL RATING Note: 1 = lowest; 5 = highest	1 2 3 4 5	1 2 3 4 5	1 2 3 4 5
NOTES:			

UNIT 4   FINAL TASK Presenting a New App

Check (✓) if the presenter:	Presenter or Group		
	_____	_____	_____
1. clearly described a new app idea	☐	☐	☐
2. discussed what the app can and can't do	☐	☐	☐
3. gave reasons why the app is useful using *because* or *since*	☐	☐	☐
4. used phrases and got his/her classmates' attention	☐	☐	☐
OVERALL RATING Note: 1 = lowest; 5 = highest	1 2 3 4 5	1 2 3 4 5	1 2 3 4 5
NOTES:			

UNIT 5   FINAL TASK Telling a Story

Check (✓) if the presenter:	Presenter or Group		
	_____	_____	_____
1. told a story about a past risk	☐	☐	☐
2. used correct forms and pronunciation of simple past	☐	☐	☐
3. gave details about the risk (why, when, how,…)	☐	☐	☐
4. asked the audience for questions during or at the end of the story	☐	☐	☐
OVERALL RATING Note: 1 = lowest; 5 = highest	1 2 3 4 5	1 2 3 4 5	1 2 3 4 5

NOTES:

UNIT 6   FINAL TASK Presenting a Project Using Images

Check (✓) if the presenter:	Presenter or Group		
	_____	_____	_____
1. presented a useful project plan to help the community	☐	☐	☐
2. used the correct forms and pronunciation of *will* or *be going to*	☐	☐	☐
3. used correct phrases to introduce sources of information	☐	☐	☐
4. used effective photos, charts, or other images to present the project plan	☐	☐	☐
OVERALL RATING Note: 1 = lowest; 5 = highest	1 2 3 4 5	1 2 3 4 5	1 2 3 4 5

NOTES:

UNIT 7   FINAL TASK Presenting a Personal History

Check (✓) if the presenter:	Presenter or Group		
	_____	_____	_____
1. presented a clear and detailed personal history	☐	☐	☐
2. used an effective timeline to present the personal history	☐	☐	☐
3. said the years or dates correctly	☐	☐	☐
4. used body language to present ideas effectively and kept audience interested	☐	☐	☐
OVERALL RATING Note: 1 = lowest; 5 = highest	1 2 3 4 5	1 2 3 4 5	1 2 3 4 5
NOTES:			

UNIT 8   FINAL TASK Group Presentation: DNA in the Real World

Check (✓) if the presenter:	Presenter or Group		
	_____	_____	_____
1. presented one way DNA is used in the real world	☐	☐	☐
2. introduced the topic clearly	☐	☐	☐
3. gave pros and cons of the use of DNA	☐	☐	☐
4. used questions to help the audience think about the topic and understand the information more easily	☐	☐	☐
OVERALL RATING Note: 1 = lowest; 5 = highest	1 2 3 4 5	1 2 3 4 5	1 2 3 4 5
NOTES:			

ACKNOWLEDGEMENTS

The Authors and Publisher would like to acknowledge the teachers around the world who participated in the development of the second edition of *Pathways*.

A special thanks to our Advisory Board for their valuable input during the development of this series.

ADVISORY BOARD

Mahmoud Al Hosni, Modern College of Business and Science, Muscat; **Safaa Al-Salim**, Kuwait University, Kuwait City; **Laila AlQadhi**, Kuwait University, Kuwait City; **Julie Bird**, RMIT University Vietnam, Ho Chi Minh City; **Elizabeth Bowles**, Virginia Tech Language and Culture Institute, Blacksburg, VA; **Rachel Bricker**, Arizona State University, Tempe, AZ; **James Broadbridge**, J.F. Oberlin University, Tokyo; **Marina Broeder**, Mission College, Santa Clara, CA; **Shawn Campbell**, Hangzhou High School, Hangzhou; **Trevor Carty**, James Cook University, Singapore; **Jindarat De Vleeschauwer**, Chiang Mai University, Chiang Mai; **Wai-Si El Hassan**, Prince Mohammad Bin Fahd University, Dhahran; **Jennifer Farnell**, University of Bridgeport, Bridgeport, CT; **Rasha Gazzaz**, King Abdulaziz University, Jeddah; **Keith Graziadei**, Santa Monica College, Santa Monica, CA; **Janet Harclerode**, Santa Monica Community College, Santa Monica, CA; **Anna Hasper**, TeacherTrain, Dubai; **Phoebe Kamel Yacob Hindi**, Abu Dhabi Vocational Education and Training Institute, Abu Dhabi; **Kuei-ping Hsu**, National Tsing Hua University, Hsinchu; **Greg Jewell**, Drexel University, Philadelphia, PA; **Adisra Katib**, Chulalongkorn University Language Institute, Bangkok; **Wayne Kennedy**, LaGuardia Community College, Long Island City, NY; **Beth Koo**, Central Piedmont Community College, Charlotte, NC; **Denise Kray**, Bridge School, Denver, CO; **Chantal Kruger**, ILA Vietnam, Ho Chi Minh City; **William P. Kyzner**, Fuyang AP Center, Fuyang; **Becky Lawrence**, Massachusetts International Academy, Marlborough, MA; **Deborah McGraw**, Syracuse University, Syracuse, NY; **Mary Moore**, University of Puerto Rico, San Juan; **Raymond Purdy**, ELS Language Centers, Princeton, NJ; **Anouchka Rachelson**, Miami Dade College, Miami, FL; **Fathimah Razman**, Universiti Utara Malaysia, Sintok; **Phil Rice**, University of Delaware ELI, Newark, DE; **Scott Rousseau**, American University of Sharjah, Sharjah; **Verna Santos-Nafrada**, King Saud University, Riyadh; **Eugene Sidwell**, American Intercon Institute, Phnom Penh; **Gemma Thorp**, Monash University English Language Centre, Melbourne; **Matt Thurston**, University of Central Lancashire, Preston; **Christine Tierney**, Houston Community College, Houston, TX; **Jet Robredillo Tonogbanua**, FPT University, Hanoi.

GLOBAL REVIEWERS

ASIA

Antonia Cavcic, Asia University, Tokyo; **Soyhan Egitim**, Tokyo University of Science, Tokyo; **Caroline Handley**, Asia University, Tokyo; **Patrizia Hayashi**, Meikai University, Urayasu; **Greg Holloway**, University of Kitakyushu, Kitakyushu; **Anne C. Ihata**, Musashino University, Tokyo; **Kathryn Mabe**, Asia University, Tokyo; **Frederick Navarro Bacala**, Yokohama City University, Yokohama; **Tyson Rode**, Meikai University, Urayasu; **Scott Shelton-Strong**, Asia University, Tokyo; **Brooks Slaybaugh**, Yokohama City University, Yokohama; **Susanto Sugiharto**, Sutomo Senior High School, Medan; **Andrew Zitzmann**, University of Kitakyushu, Kitakyushu

LATIN AMERICA AND THE CARIBBEAN

Raul Bilini, ProLingua, Dominican Republic; **Alejandro Garcia**, Collegio Marcelina, Mexico; **Humberto Guevara**, Tec de Monterrey, Campus Monterrey, Mexico; **Romina Olga Planas**, Centro Cultural Paraguayo Americano, Paraguay; **Carlos Rico-Troncoso**, Pontificia Universidad Javeriana, Colombia; **Ialê Schetty**, Enjoy English, Brazil; **Aline Simoes**, Way To Go Private English, Brazil; **Paulo Cezar Lira Torres**, APenglish, Brazil; **Rosa Enilda Vasquez**, Swisher Dominicana, Dominican Republic; **Terry Whitty**, LDN Language School, Brazil.

MIDDLE EAST AND NORTH AFRICA

Susan Daniels, Kuwait University, Kuwait; **Mahmoud Mohammadi Khomeini**, Sokhane Ashna Language School, Iran; **Müge Lenbet**, Koç University, Turkey; **Robert Anthony Lowman**, Prince Mohammad bin Fahd University, Saudi Arabia; **Simon Mackay**, Prince Mohammad bin Fahd University, Saudi Arabia.

USA AND CANADA

Frank Abbot, Houston Community College, Houston, TX; **Hossein Aksari**, Bilingual Education Institute and Houston Community College, Houston, TX; **Sudie Allen-Henn**, North Seattle College, Seattle, WA; **Sharon Allie**, Santa Monica Community College, Santa Monica, CA; **Jerry Archer**, Oregon State University, Corvallis, OR; **Nicole Ashton**, Central Piedmont Community College, Charlotte, NC; **Barbara Barrett**, University of Miami, Coral Gables, FL; **Maria Bazan-Myrick**, Houston Community College, Houston, TX; **Rebecca Beal**, Colleges of Marin, Kentfield, CA; **Marlene Beck**, Eastern Michigan University, Ypsilanti, MI; **Michelle Bell**, University of Southern California, Los Angeles, CA; **Linda Bolet**, Houston Community College, Houston, TX; **Jenna Bollinger**, Eastern Michigan University, Ypsilanti, MI; **Monica Boney**, Houston Community College, Houston, TX; **Nanette Bouvier**, Rutgers University – Newark, Newark, NJ; **Nancy Boyer**, Golden West College, Huntington Beach, CA; **Lia Brenneman**, University of Florida English Language Institute, Gainesville, FL; **Colleen Brice**, Grand Valley State University, Allendale, MI; **Kristen Brown**, Massachusetts International Academy, Marlborough, MA; **Philip Brown**, Houston Community

College, Houston, TX; **Dongmei Cao**, San Jose City College, San Jose, CA; **Molly Cheney**, University of Washington, Seattle, WA; **Emily Clark**, The University of Kansas, Lawrence, KS; **Luke Coffelt**, International English Center, Boulder, CO; **William C Cole-French**, MCPHS University, Boston, MA; **Charles Colson**, English Language Institute at Sam Houston State University, Huntsville, TX; **Lucy Condon**, Bilingual Education Institute, Houston, TX; **Janice Crouch**, Internexus Indiana, Indianapolis, IN; **Charlene Dandrow**, Virginia Tech Language and Culture Institute, Blacksburg, VA; **Loretta Davis**, Coastline Community College, Westminster, CA; **Marta Dmytrenko-Ahrabian**, Wayne State University, Detroit, MI; **Bonnie Duhart**, Houston Community College, Houston, TX; **Karen Eichhorn**, International English Center, Boulder, CO; **Tracey Ellis**, Santa Monica Community College, Santa Monica, CA; **Jennifer Evans**, University of Washington, Seattle, WA; **Marla Ewart**, Bilingual Education Institute, Houston, TX; **Rhoda Fagerland**, St. Cloud State University, St. Cloud, MN; **Kelly Montijo Fink**, Kirkwood Community College, Cedar Rapids, IA; **Celeste Flowers**, University of Central Arkansas, Conway, AR; **Kurtis Foster**, Missouri State University, Springfield, MO; **Rachel Garcia**, Bilingual Education Institute, Houston, TX; **Thomas Germain**, University of Colorado Boulder, Boulder, CO; **Claire Gimble**, Virginia International University, Fairfax, VA; **Marilyn Glazer-Weisner**, Middlesex Community College, Lowell, MA; **Amber Goodall**, South Piedmont Community College, Charlotte, NC; **Katya Goussakova**, Seminole State College of Florida, Sanford, FL; **Jane Granado**, Texas State University, San Marcos, TX; **Therea Hampton**, Mercer County Community College, West Windsor Township, NJ; **Jane Hanson**, University of Nebraska – Lincoln, Lincoln, NE; **Lauren Heather**, University of Texas at San Antonio, San Antonio, TX; **Jannette Hermina**, Saginaw Valley State University, Saginaw, MI; **Gail Hernandez**, College of Staten Island, Staten Island, NY; **Beverly Hobbs**, Clark University, Worcester, MA; **Kristin Homuth**, Language Center International, Southfield, MI; **Tim Hooker**, Campbellsville University, Campbellsville, KY; **Raylene Houck**, Idaho State University, Pocatello, ID; **Karen L. Howling**, University of Bridgeport, Bridgeport, CT; **Sharon Jaffe**, Santa Monica Community College, Santa Monica, CA; **Andrea Kahn**, Santa Monica Community College, Santa Monica, CA; **Eden Bradshaw Kaiser**, Massachusetts International Academy, Marlborough, MA; **Mandy Kama**, Georgetown University, Washington, D.C.; **Andrea Kaminski**, University of Michigan – Dearborn, Dearborn, MI; **Phoebe Kang**, Brock University, Ontario; **Eileen Kramer**, Boston University CELOP, Brookline, MA; **Rachel Lachance**, University of New Hampshire, Durham, NH; **Janet Langon**, Glendale Community College, Glendale, CA; **Frances Le Grand**, University of Houston, Houston, TX; **Esther Lee**, California State University, Fullerton, CA; **Helen S. Mays Lefal**, American Learning Institute, Dallas, TX; **Oranit Limmaneeprasert**, American River College, Sacramento, CA; **Dhammika Liyanage**, Bilingual Education Institute, Houston, TX; **Emily Lodmer**, Santa Monica Community College, Santa Monica Community College, CA; **Ari Lopez**, American Learning Institute Dallas, TX; **Nichole Lukas**, University of Dayton, Dayton, OH; **Undarmaa Maamuujav**, California State University, Los Angeles, CA; **Diane Mahin**, University of Miami, Coral Gables, FL; **Melanie Majeski**, Naugatuck Valley Community College, Waterbury, CT; **Judy Marasco**, Santa Monica Community College, Santa Monica, CA; **Murray McMahan**, University of Alberta, Alberta; **Deirdre McMurtry**, University of Nebraska Omaha, Omaha, NE; **Suzanne Meyer**, University of Pittsburgh, Pittsburgh, PA; **Cynthia Miller**, Richland College, Dallas, TX; **Sara Miller**, Houston Community College, Houston, TX; **Gwendolyn Miraglia**, Houston Community College, Houston, TX; **Katie Mitchell**, International English Center, Boulder, CO; **Ruth Williams Moore**, University of Colorado Boulder, Boulder, CO; **Kathy Najafi**, Houston Community College, Houston, TX; **Sandra Navarro**, Glendale Community College, Glendale, CA; **Stephanie Ngom**, Boston University, Boston MA; **Barbara Niemczyk**, University of Bridgeport, Bridgeport, CT; **Melody Nightingale**, Santa Monica Community College, Santa Monica, CA; **Alissa Olgun**, California Language Academy, Los Angeles, CA; **Kimberly Oliver**, Austin Community College, Austin, TX; **Steven Olson**, International English Center, Boulder, CO; **Fernanda Ortiz**, University of Arizona, Tucson, AZ; **Joel Ozretich**, University of Washington, Seattle, WA; **Erin Pak**, Schoolcraft College, Livonia, MI; **Geri Pappas**, University of Michigan – Dearborn, Dearborn, MI; **Eleanor Paterson**, Erie Community College, Buffalo, NY; **Sumeeta Patnaik**, Marshall University, Huntington, WV; **Mary Peacock**, Richland College, Dallas, TX; **Kathryn Porter**, University of Houston, Houston, TX; **Eileen Prince**, Prince Language Associates, Newton Highlands, MA; **Marina Ramirez**, Houston Community College, Houston, TX; **Laura Ramm**, Michigan State University, East Lansing, MI; **Chi Rehg**, University of South Florida, Tampa, FL; **Cyndy Reimer**, Douglas College, New Westminster, British Columbia; **Sydney Rice**, Imperial Valley College, Imperial, CA; **Lynnette Robson**, Mercer University, Macon, GA; **Helen E. Roland**, Miami Dade College, Miami, FL; **Maria Paula Carreira Rolim**, Southeast Missouri State University, Cape Girardeau, MO; **Jill Rolston-Yates**, Texas State University, San Marcos, TX; **David Ross**, Houston Community College, Houston, TX; **Rachel Scheiner**, Seattle Central College, Seattle, WA; **John Schmidt**, Texas Intensive English Program, Austin, TX; **Mariah Schueman**, University of Miami, Coral Gables, FL; **Erika Shadburne**, Austin Community College, Austin, TX; **Mahdi Shamsi**, Houston Community College, Houston, TX; **Osha Sky**, Highline College, Des Moines, WA; **William Slade**, University of Texas, Austin, TX; **Takako Smith**, University of Nebraska – Lincoln, Lincoln, NE; **Barbara Smith-Palinkas**, Hillsborough Community College, Tampa, FL; **Paula Snyder**, University of Missouri, Columbia, MO; **Mary; Evelyn Sorrell**, Bilingual Education Institute, Houston TX; **Kristen Stauffer**, International English Center, Boulder, CO; **Christina Stefanik**, The Language Company, Toledo, OH; **Cory Stewart**, University of Houston, Houston, TX; **Laurie Stusser-McNeill**, Highline College, Des Moines, WA; **Tom Sugawara**, University of Washington, Seattle, WA; **Sara Sulko**, University of Missouri, Columbia, MO; **Mark Sullivan**, University of Colorado Boulder, Boulder, CO; **Olivia Szabo**, Boston University, Boston, MA; **Amber Tallent**, University of Nebraska Omaha, Omaha, NE; **Amy Tate**, Rice University, Houston, USA; **Aya C. Tiacoh**, Bilingual Education Institute, Houston, TX; **Troy Tucker**, Florida SouthWestern State College, Fort Myers, FL; **Anne Tyoan**, Savannah College of Art and Design, Savannah, GA; **Michael Vallee**, International English Center, Boulder, CO; **Andrea Vasquez**, University of Southern Maine, Portland, ME; **Jose Vasquez**, University of Texas Rio Grande Valley, Edinburgh, TX; **Maureen Vendeville**, Savannah Technical College, Savannah, GA; **Melissa Vervinck**, Oakland University, Rochester, MI; **Adriana Villarreal**, Universided Nacional Autonoma de Mexico, San Antonio, TX; **Summer Webb**, International English Center, Boulder, CO; **Mercedes Wilson-Everett**, Houston Community College, Houston, TX; **Lora Yasen**, Tokyo International University of America, Salem, OR; **Dennis Yommer**, Youngstown State University, Youngstown, OH; **Melojeane (Jolene) Zawilinski**, University of Michigan – Flint, Flint, MI.

CREDITS

PHOTOS

Cover ©Spencer Black

iv BEHROUZ MEHRI/Getty Images, **iv** ©Jim Richardson/National Geographic Creative, **iv** Lars Ruecker/Getty Images, **iv** Jeff J Mitchell/Getty Images, **iv** ©Thomas P. Peschak/National Geographic Creative, **vi** ©NASA/National Geographic Creative, **vi** Javier Jaen/National Geographic Creative, **vi** Cultura RM / Alamy Stock Photo, **Contents Page** ©Spencer Black, **1** (c) BEHROUZ MEHRI/Getty Images, **2** (bl) isitsharp/Getty Images, **3** (t) ©Tino Soriano/National Geographic Creative, **3** (cr) ©WILLIAM ALBERT ALLARD/National Geographic Creative, **3** (bl) ©Adam Kokot/Aurora Photos, **4** (cr) valentinrussanov/Getty Images, **4** (cr) WAYHOME studio/Shutterstock.com, **6** (c) Dimitri Otis/Getty Images, **8** (c) ©Chris Bashinelli/National Geographic Creative, **9** (t) Chris Bashinelli, **12** (t) LYNN JOHNSON/National Geographic Creative, **12** (br) Cengage Learning, Inc., **14–15** (b) ©Aaron Joel Santos/Aurora Photos, **16** (bc) Cengage Learning, Inc., **19** (c) ©Jason Edwards/National Geographic Creative, **21** (c) ©Jim Richardson/National Geographic Creative, **22–23** (c) Jianan Yu/Reuters, **24** (bc) ©Deanne Fitzmaurice/National Geographic Creative, **26** (bc) VCG/Getty Images, **30** (b) Reza/Getty Images, **32** (t) ©Don Wilson, **34–35** (b) ©NACHO DOCE/REUTERS, **36** (bc) dotshock/Shutterstock.com, **38** (cl) Hulton Archive/Getty Images, **38** (cr) Eamonn McCormack/Getty Images, **38** (c) ©Nathan Lazarnick/George Eastman House/Getty Images, **41** (c) Lars Ruecker/Getty Images, **42–43** (c) ©O Chul Kwon, **43** (br) ©Stringer/Reuters, **43** (tr) Westend61/Getty Images, **44** (b) Mlenny/Getty Images, **46** (c) Cengage Learning, Inc., **46** (bc) XPACIFICA/National Geographic Creative, **46** (tl) Chanwit Issarasuwipakorn/Shutterstock.com, **46** (tr) QMTstudio/Shutterstock.com, **48–49** (b) ©PANORAMIC IMAGES/National Geographic Creative, **51** (cl) National Geographic Creative/Alamy Stock Photo, **51** (cr) RALPH LEE HOPKINS/National Geographic Creative, **51** (cr) Edwin Verin/Shutterstock.com, **52** (cr) Cengage Learning, Inc., **52** (t) StoryLife / Alamy Stock Photo, **54** (bc) ©MAGGIE STEBER/National Geographic Creative, **56** (b) E.D. Torial / Alamy Stock Photo, **56** (cr) Cengage Learning, Inc., **61** (c) Jeff J Mitchell/Getty Images, **62** (cl) The Protected Art Archive / Alamy Stock Photo, **62** (cr) Jenny Bohr/Alamy Stock Photo, **62** (bl) David Lees/Getty Images, **62** (br) Warren Diggles / Alamy Stock Photo, **62–63** (c) Ramiro Torrents/Getty Images, **63** (cl) Ian Shaw/Alamy Stock Photo, **63** (cl) Tomasz Zajda/Alamy Stock Photo, **64** (bc) MARC MORITSCH/National Geographic Creative, **66** (cl) CHIH YUAN Ronnie Wu/Alamy Stock Photo, **66** (cr) New photos by Alfonso de Tomas / Alamy Stock Photo, **68** (c) ©Kuri/Mayfield Robotics, **69** (bc) ©xPACIFICA/Aurora Photos, **70** (b) New York Daily News Archive/Getty Images, **72** (c) Cengage Learning, Inc., **72** (t) ©Christher Kimmel/Aurora Photos, **75** (t) NOEL CELIS/Getty Images, **76** (bc) ©Amelia Fletcher/Aurora Photos, **81** (c) ©Thomas P. Peschak/National Geographic Creative, **82–083** (c) MIKEY SCHAEFER/National Geographic Creative, **83** (tr) ©Mattias Klum/National Geographic Creative, **83** (br) ALEX TREADWAY/National Geographic Creative, **85** (t) Tommy Heinrich/National Geographic Creative, **86** (t) AARON HUEY/National Geographic Creative, **86** (cr) PRAKASH MATHEMA/Getty Images, **89** (bc) Mauricio Graiki/Shutterstock, **90** (cr) Steve Vidler / Alamy Stock Photo, **90** (cl) naito29/Shutterstock, **90** (bl) foodfolio / Alamy Stock Photo, **90** (br) Bloomberg/Getty Images, **092** (br) Cengage Learning, Inc., **92** (t) ©Mikey Schaefer, **95** (bc) ©Joel Sartore/National Geographic Creative, **96** (cr) ©Mark Thiessen/National Geographic Creative, **96** (bc) Michael Nichols/National Geographic Creative, **96** (cl) Cengage Learning, Inc., **99** (bc) Rolf Nussbaumer Photography / Alamy Stock Photo, **101** (c) ©NASA/National Geographic Creative, **102** (br) Texturis/Shutterstock, **102–103** (c) Paul Kennedy/Getty Images, **103** (b) JIANG HONGYAN/Shutterstock, **103** (b) photosync/Shutterstock, **103** (tr) Mariyana M/Shutterstock, **103** (b) AlenKadr/Shutterstock, **104** (bl) Mariyana M/Shutterstock, **104** (cr) hidesy/Shutterstock, **104** (c) PJjaruwan/Shutterstock, **104** (bc) Alfazet Chronicles/Shutterstock, **104** (br) SpeedKingz/Shutterstock, **106** (tr) ©National Geographic Maps, **106** (b) BIOSPHOTO/Alamy Stock Photo, **109** (b) Federico Rostagno / Alamy Stock Photo, **111** (b) Hero Images Inc. / Alamy Stock Photo, **112** (tl) KATE THOMPSON/National Geographic Creative, **112** (tr) PETE MCBRIDE/National Geographic Creative, **114** (tc) ©Joel Sartore/National Geographic Creative, **115** (bc) The Washington Post/Getty Images, **116** (tr) ©Nalini Nadkarni, **117** (t) ©Benjamin Drummond, **120** (tr) Ben Birchall - PA Images/Getty Images, **120** (cr) jeremy sutton-hibbert/Alamy Stock Photo, **120** (cr) ©National Geographic Learning, **121** (c) Javier Jaen/National Geographic Creative;, **122** (br) Chronicle / Alamy Stock Photo, **122** (bl) ©Kenneth Garrett/National Geographic Creative, **122–123** (c) ©James L. Stanfield/National Geographic Creative, **123** (br) age fotostock / Alamy Stock Photo, **123** (bl) Vespasian / Alamy Stock Photo, **123** (t) Cengage Learning, Inc., **124** (b) Henry Groskinsky/Getty Images, **126** (bc) Iakov Filimonov/Shutterstock, **130** (t) EMORY KRISTOF/National Geographic Creative, **132** (cr) Cengage Learning, Inc., **132** (t) ©Kat Keene Hogue/National Geographic Creative, **133** (bc) ©Rebecca Hale/National Geographic Creative, **134–135** (b) MuseoPics - Paul Williams / Alamy Stock Photo, **136** (b) www.BibleLandPictures.com / Alamy Stock Photo, **138** (b) JONATHAN KINGSTON/National Geographic Creative, **141** (c) Cultura RM / Alamy Stock Photo, **142–143** (c) ©Stocktrek Images/National Geographic Creative, **144** (b) ©Kevin Horan/Aurora Photos, **146** (bc) ©Stocktrek Images/National Geographic Creative, **148** (b) ©Richard Olsenius/National Geographic Creative, **149** (t) Oxana Oleynichenko / Alamy Stock Photo, **152** (t) Brent Stirton/Getty Images, **153** (t) MATT CHWASTYK/National Geographic Creative, **154** (c) Bloomberg/Getty Images, **154** (bc) John Greim/Getty Images, **155** (t) TINO SORIANO/National Geographic, **156** (bc) Ralph C. Eagle, Jr./Science Source, **158** (bc) ©Jason Treat/National Geographic Creative, **159** (t) ©Isabella Apriyana/National Geographic Creative, **161** Cultura RM / Alamy Stock Photo,

LISTENING AND TEXT SOURCES

6–7: Sources: Live Science, "Twins Separated at Birth Reveal Staggering Influence of Genetics" by Tanya Lewis; Minnesota Center for Twin & Family Research, "Other Twin Research at the U of M" by The Regents of the University of Minnesota Website; First to Know, "The Remarkable 'Jim Twins': Separated at Birth, They Shared the Same Life" by Jeffery Rindskopf; **14:** Sources: https://en.wikipedia.org/wiki/List_of_average _human_height_worldwide, Women's News Network Global, "Afghanistan: Large families encouraged by culture as well as religion" by Aunohita Mojumdar; The Japan Times, "Japanese women No. 1 in worldwide life expectancy for third straight year" by Kyodo; https:// en.wikipedia.org/wiki/Age_of_majority, United States Census Bureau, "The Majority of Children Live With Two Parents, Census Bureau Reports" by United States Census Bureau; World Family Map 2014, "Family Structure" by The World Family Map c/o Child Trends; Between Us Parents, "10 interesting stats about teens, technology and social media usage" by Shannan Younger; U.S. News, "Countries Where the Most Young Adults Live With Their Parents" by Devon Haynie; **16:** Source: PBS, "Inside the Teenage Brain" by WGBH educational foundation; **17:** Sources: National Institute of Mental Health, "The Teen Brain: 6 Things to Know" by National Institutes of Health; PBS, "Anatomy of a Teen Brain" by WGBH educational foundation; PBS, "Inside the Teenage Brain" by WGBH educational foundation; **23:** Source: happify daily, "How to Beat Stress and Boost Happiness" by happify; **24:** Sources: The Society for Human Resource Management, "Employee Job Satisfaction and Engagement: Revitalizing a Changing Workforce" by The Society for Human Resource Management; Inc.com, "The U.S. Now Has 27 Million Entrepreneurs" by Leigh Buchanan; **38:** Source: visually, "People Who Found Success Despite Failures" by ohnoitsfab http://visual.ly/people-who-found-success -despite-failures; **47:** Source: Atlas Obscura, "Lotus Lake" by charles; **56–57:** Sources: ICEHOTEL "ICEHOTEL" http://icehotel.co.uk/, Nordic Visitor Travel Experts, "ICEHOTEL Winter Adventure" by Nordic Visitor Travel Experts; **68:** © 2017 Mayfield Robotics. https://www.heykuri.com /living-with-a-personal-robot; **75:** Sources: BGR, "Horrifying chart reveals how much time we spend staring at screens each day" by Zach Epstein http://bgr.com/2014/05/29/smartphone-computer-usage-study-chart/; infoplease "How People Use Their Cell Phones" by infoplease http://www.factmonster.com/ipka/A0933561.html; **76–77:** Sources: Huffington Post, "You Probably Use Your Smartphone Way More Than You Think" by Carolyn Gregorie; The New York Times, "How Walking in Nature Changes the Brain" by Gretchen Reynolds; **86:** Sources: National Geographic, "Meet the 10 Most Inspiring Adventurers of the Year" by National Geographic Partners, LLC; National Geographic, "Mountaineer Pasang Lhamu Sherpa Akita" by National Geographic Partners, LLC; **90:** Source: National Geographic, "11 Daring Dishes to Eat" by National Geographic Partners, LLC; **96:** Source: National Geographic, "Emma Stokes" by National Geographic Partners, LLC; **103:** Sources: National Geographic, "Pollution" by National Geographic Society https://www.nationalgeographic.org/encyclopedia/pollution/; New Hampshire Department of Environmental Services, "Time it takes for garbage to decompose in the environment"; **104:** Sources: project: greenify, "9 Easy Ways to Use Less Plastic" by bounceenergy; ABC News, "Study: Bottled Water No Safer Than Tap Water" by Mark Baumgartner; **106–107:** Sources: National Geographic Education Blog, "The Great Pacific Garbage Patch" by ngeducationteam; EcoWatch, "22 Facts About Plastic Pollution (And 10 Things We Can Do About It)" by Nicole D'Alessandro; The Guardian, "Collecting plastic waste near coasts 'is most effective clean-up method'" by Rebecca Smithers; **109:** Sources: inhabitat, "China's first vertical forest is rising in Nanjing," by Lacy Cooke; Mestna občina Ljubljana, "Ljubljana. For you." by Mestna občina Ljubljana http://www.greenljubljana.com; **115:** Source: The Evergreen State College and Washington State Department of Corrections, "Sustainability in Prisons Project" by The Evergreen State College and Washington State Department of Corrections; **116:** Sources: National Geographic, "5 Unconventional Ways to Get People Hooked on Nature" by Christine Dell'Amore; National Geographic, "NG Live!: Nalini Nadkarni: For the Love of Trees" by National Geographic Live! National Geographic, "Biologist Wants Nature for Everyone - Including Prisoners" by Gary Strauss; **122–123:** Source: St. Catharine's Standard, "Niagara's Most Famous Mummy" by Laura Ranieri; **124:** Sources: The Telegraph, "The hunt for the million-dollar Faberge eggs" by Lucinda Everett; Fabergé, "The Impterial Eggs" by Fabergé; **126–127:** Source: NPR, "Seeking Adventure And Gold? Crack This Poem And Head Outdoors" by John Burnett; **129:** Source: joeccombs2nd, "Lost Ships of the 1715 Spanish Treasure Fleet (Lost Treasures Part 4)" by COMBS2JC https://joeccombs2nd.com/2014/08/03 /lost-ships-of-the-1715-spanish-treasure-fleet-lost-treasures-part-4/; **130:** Source: LOLWOT, "20 Real Lost Treasures Hidden Around the World" by LOLWOT http://www.lolwot.com/20-real-lost-treasures-hidden-around-the-world/; **136–137:** Source: Iran Heritage Foundation America, "What is the Cyrus Cylinder?" by IHF America; **142–143:** Source: Owlcation, "How to Explain DNA to Kids" by Rhys Baker https://owlcation. com/academia/explaining-dna-to-a-six-year-old; **146:** Sources: History.com, "Why did the dinosaurs die out?" by History.com staff; National Geographic, "Bringing Them Back to Life" by Carl Zimmer; ScienceDaily, "Nottingham Dollies prove cloned sheep can live long and healthy lives" by ScienceDaily; **148:** Sources: Texas A&M Today, "Some Paws for Celebration: World's First Cloned Cat Turns 15 at Texas A&M" by Keith Randall http://today.tamu.edu/2017/03/23/some-paws-for-celebration-worlds-first-cloned-cat-turns-15-at-texas-am/; ScienceDaily, "Texas A&M Clones First Cat" by ScienceDaily; **150:** Sources: National Geographic, "Scientists Successfully Clone Cat" by David Braun; Popular Science, "The 11 Most Important Cats of Science" by Sarah Fecht; **152:** Source: See International, "Dr. Helena Ndume – 35,000 Surgeries & Counting" https://www.seeintl.org/ndume/; **154:** Source: Forbes.com, "No Donor Required: 5 Body Parts You Can Make With 3-D Printers" by Robert J. Szczerba; **156:** Sources: National Geographic, "Why There's New Hope About Ending Blindness" by David Dobbs; Learn.Genetics, "Amazing Cells" by Learn.Genetics Genetic Science Learning Center http://learn.genetics.utah.edu/content/cells/; The Free Dictionary, "Cell Therapy" by The Free Dictionary http://medical-dictionary.thefreedictionary.com/Cell+Therapy; **156–157:** Sources: National Geographic, "Why There's New Hope About Ending Blindness" by David Dobbs; World Health Organization, "Visual impairment and blindness" by World Health Organization http://www.who.int/mediacentre/factsheets/fs282/en/; **158:** National Geographic, "How Science is Putting a New Face on Crime Solving" by Veronique Greenwood.

INDEX OF EXAM SKILLS AND TASKS

Pathways Listening, Speaking, and Critical Thinking, 2nd Edition, is designed to provide practice for standardized exams, such as IELTS and TOEFL. Many activities in this book practice or focus on **key exam skills** needed for test success. Here is an index of activities in Level Foundations that are similar to **common questions types** found in these tests.

Listening

Key Exam Skills	IELTS	TOEFL	Page and Exercise/Skill Box
Activating prior knowledge	X	X	16 A, 26 A, 36 A, 46 A, 106 A, 146 A
Identifying main ideas	X	X	17 LS, 17 C, 26 B, 36 B, 47 C, 56 B, 66 B, 76 B, 86 B, 97 B, 106 C, 116 B, 126 B, 136 B, 146 B, 156 B
Listening actively (by predicting)	X	X	56 A, 106 B, 126 A, 156 A
Listening for a speaker's attitude / emotions	X		107 LS, 107 F, 107 G
Listening for examples	X	X	87 LS, 87 C
Listening for key details	X	X	6 D, 17 D, 26 C, 27 E, 36 C, 47 LS, 47 E, 67 D, 76 C, 87 D, 97 C, 109 C, 116 C, 137 C, 146 C, 157 D
Listening for opinions	X	X	147 LS, 147 D, 150 D
Listening for pros and cons	X	X	147 E
Listening for signposts or steps in a process	X	X	27 LS, 27 D, 67 LS, 67 C
Listening for supporting examples	X	X	87 LS
Listening for reasons and explanations	X	X	127 LS, 127 C
Making inferences	X	X	57 D
Organizing the notes you take	X	X	77 NT, 77 D, 137 NT, 137 D, 147 NT, 147 E
Reviewing your notes	X	X	97 NTB, 97 E
Taking notes on key words and phrases	X	X	37 D, 97 D
Using abbreviations when taking notes	X	X	107 NT, 107 E
Using diagrams when taking notes	X	X	7 NT, 7 E
Taking notes on questions you hear	X	X	57 NT, 57 C

Common Question Types for Listening	IELTS	TOEFL	Page and Exercise
Multiple response		X	17 C
Matching	X		37 E, 47 E, 109 D
Multiple choice	X	X	17 C, 56 B, 66 B, 67 D, 86 B, 87 D, 97 B, 116 C, 136 B, 137 C
Sentence completion	X		27 D, 36 C, 67 C, 87 C, 147 D
Short answer	X		27 E
Table completion	X		127 C, 157 C

SKILL-BOX KEY

LS — Listening Skill
NT — Note-Taking Skill

Speaking

Key Exam Skills	IELTS	TOEFL	Page and Exercise/Skill Box
Brainstorming ideas	X	X	80 B, 100 A, 119 A, 139 B, 149 B, 159 B
Categorizing information	X	X	30 CT, 30 I, 31 B, 31 C, 55 E, 91 A
Concluding a talk or speech	X	X	40 PS
Discussing plans and ideas	X	X	91 A, 91 C
Discussing problems and solutions	X	X	111 C
Discussing pros and cons	X	X	35 D, 37 G, 50 CT, 50 E, 50 F, 53 G, 59 C, 149 C
Expressing agreement or disagreement	X	X	48 SS, 48 B, 150 EL, 151 B
Expressing opinions	X	X	17 E, 37 F, 51 C, 55 F, 67 E, 77 E, 90 H, 95 F, 125 E, 147 F, 150 SS, 151 A
Expressing possibility	X	X	148 GFS, 157 F
Giving supporting examples	X	X	90 SS, 90 G, 91 A
Giving reasons for an opinion	X	X	31 C, 51 C, 57 D, 65 E, 70 SS, 70 D, 73 G, 90 H, 95 F, 115 E, 135 E
Interpreting diagrams and visuals[1]	X		16 B, 24 B, 47 B, 75 CT, 75 D
Making eye contact	X		20 PS
Making predictions	X	X	118 GFS, 118 A, 118 B
Mentioning your sources	X	X	110 SS, 110 E, 110 G, 111 C
Organizing your ideas when you speak	X	X	20 B, 40 C, 100 B, 139 C, 160 C
Pronouncing the ends of words clearly	X	X	29 PRON, 29 E, 29 G, 99 PRON, 99 B, 99 C
Saying years correctly	X	X	130 SS, 131 E, 131 C, 131 D
Speaking about habits	X	X	105 E, 110 F
Paraphrasing what you have heard		X	93 CT, 93 E
Talking about abstract concepts	X		13 H, 19 A, 39 C, 53 F, 65 E, 85 E, 87 E, 93 F, 95 D, 115 E, 137 E
Talking about a chart or graph	X		60 E, 75 D, 75 E
Talking about hypothetical situations	X	X	135 E
Talking about yourself, your life, or your job	X		10 SS, 25 E, 27 F, 31 D, 33 F, 39 B, 40 F, 140 E
Talking about technology	X	X	71 A, 71 B, 77 E, 79 C, 79 D, 80 C
Telling a personal story	X	X	100 C
Using contractions and reductions naturally	X	X	18 PRON, 18 A, 18 C, 108 PRON, 108 B
Using correct stress	X	X	58 PRON, 58 A, 58 B, 158 PRON, 158 A
Using effective body language	X		140 PS
Using listing words	X	X	38 SS, 38 A
Using and pronouncing modals correctly	X	X	68 GFS, 68 PRON, 68 A, 69 B, 69 C

SKILL-BOX KEY

CT	Critical Thinking
EL	Everyday Language
GFS	Grammar for Speaking
PRON	Pronunciation
PS	Presentation Skill
SS	Speaking Skill

Pathways	CEFR	IELTS Band	TOEFL Score
Level 4	C1	65–70	81–100
Level 3	B2	55–60	51–80
Level 2	B1–B2	45–50	31–50
Level 1	A2–B1	0–40	0–30
Foundations	**A1–A2**		